By Christopher Dow

Fiction
Effigy
    Book I: Stroud
    Book II: Oakdale
The Books of Bob
    Devil of a Time
    Jumping Jehovah
The Clay Guthrie Mysteries
    The Dead Detective
    Landscape with Beast
    The Texas Troll Unlimited
Roadkill
The Werewolf and Tide, and other Compulsions

Nonfiction
Lord of the Loincloth (nonfiction novel)
Book of Curiosities: Adventures in the Paranormal
Occasional Pilgrimage: Essays on Film, Literature, and Other Matters
Living the Story: The Meandering, True, and Sometimes Strange
    Adventures of an Unknown Writer
    Vol.I: Growing Up Takes a Long Time
    Vol. II: Growing Old Takes Longer

Martial Arts
The Wellspring: An Inquiry into the Nature of Chi
Circling the Square: Observations on the Dynamics of Tai Chi Chuan
Elements of Power: Essays on the Art and Practice of Tai Chi Chuan
Alchemy of Breath: An Introduction to Chi Kung
Leaves on the Wind: A Survey of Martial Arts Literature (Vols. I-VII)

Poetry
City of Dreams
The Trip Out
Texas White Line Fever
Networks
A Dilapidation of Machinery
Puzzle Pieces: Selected Poems

Editor
The Abby Stone: The Poetry of Bartholo Dias
The Best of Phosphene
The Best of Dialog

LEAVES ON THE WIND

Volume II

LEAVES ON THE WIND

A Survey of Martial Arts Literature

Volume II

Chi Kung, Meditation, Yoga,
Archery, Research Resources,
Film & Television,
Booklets & Pamphlets

CHRISTOPHER DOW

Phosphene Publishing Company
Temple, Texas

Leaves on the Wind: A Survey of Martial Arts Literature, Volume II

© 2022 by Christopher Dow
ISBN: 978-1-7369307-6-2

All rights reserved. This work may not be copied or otherwise produced or reproduced, in whole or in part, in any form, printed or electronic, without express permission from the publisher, except for brief excerpts used in reviews, articles, and critical works.

Published by:
Phosphene Publishing Company
Temple, Texas, USA
phosphenepublishing.com

1.1

LEAVES ON THE WIND

Volume II

Contents

Part I: Chi Kung

    Chi Kung: Health & Martial Arts——15
        Yang Jwing-ming

    The Book of Internal Exercises——21
        Stephen T. Chang with Richard C. Miller

    The Chinese Way to a Long and Healthy Life: Diet, Exercise, Massage——23
        Compiled and Edited by the People's Medical Publishing House

    The Chinese Way to Family Health & Fitness: Wushu!——25
        The People's Sports Publishing House (Selected and translated by Timothy Tung)

    Self Healing: Chinese Exercises for Health and Longevity——27
        Erle Montaigue

    Prolonging Life: Ridding Illness without Medicine——29
        Yin Qianhe

    The Art of Breathing: Thirty Simple Exercises for Improving Your Performance and Well-being——33
        Nancy Zi

    The Chi Revolution: Harness the Healing Power of Your Life Force——37
        Bruce Frantzis

    The Tao of Health and Longevity——39
        Da Liu

    Kunwu Sword Neigong——43
        Jiang Rongqiao

    An Authentic Depiction of Damo's Yijinjing——47
        Jin Ti'an

A Handbook for Twelve-Posture Yijinjing——49
A Handbook for Twenty-Four-Posture Yijinjing
    Wang Huaiqi

Scientific Martial Arts——51
    Wu Zhiqing

Fitness Techniques on a Bed——55
Scientific Baduanjin
    Yin Qianhe

The Luohan Exercises——59
    Xu Longhou

Wisdom of the Luohans of the Western Regions——61
    The Daoist Shengxiao

The Luohan Exercises——63
    Huang Hanxun

An Authentic Depiction of Yue Fei's Baduanjin——65
    Jin Ti'an

The Warrior Athlete: Mind, Body & Spirit——67
    Dan Millman

Part II: Meditation

On Silent Meditation——79
    Wan Laisheng

The Tao of Meditation: Way to Enlightenment——81
    Jou Tsung Hwa

Meditation: An Eight-Point Program——89
    Eknath Easwaran

Part III: Yoga

Yoga Made Easy: A Personal Yoga Program that Will Transform Your Daily Life——97
    Howard Kent

Weight Control through Yoga——99
    Richard L. Hittleman

Part IV: Archery

> Archery Principles——105
>> Qi Jiguang (and Yu Dayou)
>
> Archery——107
>> Wayne C. McKinney
>
> Encyclopedia of Archery——111
>> W. F. Paterson

Part V: Research Resources

> Acupuncture Medicine: Its Historical and Clinical Background——115
>> Yoshiaki Omura, ScD, MD
>
> The Body Electric: Electromagnetism and the Foundation of Life——119
>> Robert O. Becker, M.D., and Gary Selden
>
> The Second Brain: A Groundbreaking New Understanding of Nervous Disorders of the Stomach and Intestines——121
>> Michael D. Gershon, M.D.
>
> The Electrical Activity of the Nervous System: A Textbook for Students——125
>> Mary A. B. Brazier
>
> Chinese Martial Arts Training Manuals: A Historical Survey——127
>> Brian Kennedy and Elizabeth Guo
>
> Not Lost in Translation——143
>> Brennan Translations

Part VI: Film & Television

> Kung Fu: Cinema of Vengeance——151
>> Verina Glaessner
>
> Martial Arts Movies: From Bruce Lee to the Ninjas——155
>> Richard Meyers, Amy Harlib, and Bill and Karen Palmer
>
> The Kung Fu Book of Caine: The Complete Guide to TV's First Mystical Eastern Western——165
>> Herbie J. Pilato

Part VII: Booklets & Pamphlets

Tai Chi Chuan——175
  Her Yue Wong

William Chen's Tai Chi Chuan——177
  William C. C. Chen

Quick and Easy T'ai-chi Ch'uan: Eight Simple Chinese Exercises for Health——179
  Yang Ming-shih

Pa-Kua: The Gentle Art of Health——181
  John Painter

Dragonbolt: A Bora-Yong (Purple Dragon) Self-defense Course——185
  D. H. Elder, Jr.

Tai Chi Sabre for Self-defense——187
  Tom Marks (ed.)

Chen Taijiquan: The Inner Circle of Secrecy——191
  Michael A. DeMarco

Li Li Ta Scrapbook——197
  Li Li Ta

PART I

Chi Kung

Chi Kung
Health & Martial Arts

By Yang Jwing-ming
(Yang's Martial Arts Academy, 1985, 122 pages)

Yang Jwing-ming, is a true master of the Chinese martial arts, with expertise in White Crane, Taiji, Chin Na, and other kung fu styles, and he has written extensively on those subjects. But in *Chi Kung: Health & Martial Arts*, he tacks slightly to the side of the martial arts to discuss the associated arts of chi kung and meditation.

Chi kung attracted greater attention in the two decades following the roll over of the millennium, but when Yang published this book in 1985, the subject was relatively new to the West. For those still new to it, "chi kung" is an umbrella term for various exercises designed to stimulate and build the chi—the intrinsic internal energy—so that it can be used for various purposes. Those purposes fall into two major categories: increasing martial power and enhancing health and well-being, often with significant overlapping effects between the two.

As there are literally thousands of chi kung movements, an overwhelming assortment presents itself to the novice. Indeed, chi kung exercises have become so numerous and diverse as they continue to branch from their root that they sometimes don't seem to be in the same class of exercises as one other. They do, in fact, require their own taxonomy, some of which Yang lays out in this excellent primer for the concepts of chi and chi kung by an acknowledged and generous master.

After some short prefatory material, the book opens with an introduction of the basic terms and concepts of chi kung—including the superstitious mindset that surrounded the art in the past. Overarching all is the idea of the chi, which is defined as an element of the life force—one that connects the spirit with the flesh. It is an ever-present component that, like the flesh, can be enhanced, strengthened, and willfully directed. Among chi kung's terms and concepts is the idea of the chi meridians—the channels in the human body through which the chi flows—and cavities. Cavities are places where the meridians run close to the surface, usually at dimples or dips in the flesh, such as the solar plexus or the little dent on the inner side of the upper arm, between the bicep and tricep.

A brief discussion of yin/yang theory and the Five Elements theory leads to a section on the division of chi kung into two different schools: Wai Dan, or external chi kung, and Nei Dan, or internal chi kung. Obviously these roughly coincide, respectively, with Shaolin kung fu styles and the Wudang arts of Taiji, Bagua, Xingyi, and so forth. Yang includes Liuhebafa (Water Boxing) in his discussions of Wudang styles.

A historical survey comes next, and it is an interesting read. Most martial arts books relate a history of the martial arts, beginning with the Indian sage, Bodhidharma (Damo) bringing Buddhism and the rudiments of kung fu to the Shaolin Temple. They then continue with the spread of those two practices throughout China and to the neighboring nations and cultures of Japan, Korea, Okinawa, and so forth. Thus, most martial arts history is presented from a martial arts perspective and often ignores the already present nascent martial arts—and their associated arts—that already existed in China and other countries.

This book approaches the same material from a a different standpoint, revealing interesting aspects of martial arts history through its depiction of the development of chi kung and traditional Chinese medicine (TCM). Also there is a nicely detailed breakdown of how Buddhism spread and evolved. In addition, Yang begins at an earlier date than do most writers, with Bodhidharma appearing only about a third of the way into the several-page history. The upshot is that the author's focus is not on the way

Bodhidharma's teachings seeded the kung fu arts tree, but on the development of the major branch that unfurled into the two branches of chi kung and traditional Chinese medicine (TCM).

Yang's version version of the Bodhidharma story is more rational than those relayed by most authors. While he gives several background details about the sage, his account, as with all historical accounts based primarily on legend, is in question—and so is the actual existence of Bodhidharma, which Yang recognizes. In any case, he says, Damo is like some characters in dramas based on real life: an amalgam of several individuals—in this case, the many people who contributed to the migration of Buddhism from India to China and to the subsequent rise of the Shaolin martial arts. But let's not quibble. Martial arts stories and legends—China's "Wild History"—are part and parcel of martial arts lore, and they have powerful connections to human archetypes, so we all tend to go along with them whether we believe them or not.

Chapter two covers Wai Dan, or external chi kung, which usually is associated with Shaolin-style kung fu. This type of chi kung tends to use repetitive muscular contraction to bring chi to one area of the body or another for specific martial purposes or simply to then let it overflow from its source area into the meridian system as a whole. The earliest-known form of this is Damo's Yi Gin Ching, a set of several movements that eventually morphed into the well-known Wai Dan chi kung known as the Eight Pieces of Brocade.

After a bit of textual instruction that includes hints, tips, and a few warnings and prohibitions, Yang (or sometimes a student) demonstrates five chi kung forms, some simple, others somewhat more complex. Yang's version of the Eight Pieces of Brocade is included—I say "version" because it seems that everyone performs this set of exercises slightly differently. The textual instructions are good, and so are the photographs. You could easily learn these exercises from the instructions.

Chapter three takes on the more extensive and deeper subject of Nei Dan, or internal chi kung. The introductory material covers the basic aspects of chi development and movement, but before Yang gets to the meat of these matters, he gives the background of Nei Dan, which necessarily includes delving into the four major martial arts expressed through internal means: Taiji, Bagua, Xingyi, and Liuhebafa.

This is followed by a discussion of principles. Each school—Wai Dan and Nei Dan—has advantages and disadvantages. Because Wai Dan tend to follow repetitive patterns in a way similar to calisthenics or yoga, they are easier to learn. Also, it is relatively simple to build up localized chi, so even short-term practice produces improved health and localized power that can be easily applied martially.

Nei Dan, on the other hand, tends to be more difficult to learn because the internal results cannot be perceived for a relatively longer period of time. However, when they are perceived, they are systemic rather than localized, flowing through and affecting the entire body. That perception leads to the concept of willful control over the flow. Because the effects of Nei Dan are systemic, these exercises generally require qualified instruction, patience, and caution to avoid excesses or stagnations of chi. Once the circulation of chi is complete and perceived and the practitioner gains some measure of willful control over it, the chi thus developed is much more powerful for martial purposes than that generated by Wai Dan exercises.

In the end, many martial artists practice a little of both types, and that tends to be the modern take on matters, but the methodology of Nei Dan exercises, which is Yang's next subject, remains old-school. The human body hasn't changed much over the last couple of centuries, and methods to stimulate the chi that worked back in the day still work now. This section contains a great deal of good information about Nei Dan, including extensive discussions of the various channels of the meridian system, how the system functions, and many important acupressure points along the meridians that are useful for a martial artist to know. The text is supplemented by many illustrations depicting the principal meridians, with important points noted.

Next, Yang describes an exercise designed to dramatically increase the chi flow through the Small Circulation (Governing Vessel + Conception Vessel). This instruction is for those who do not yet have awareness of the flow. Next is a discussion of the idea that the chi circulating through the meridians is most vulnerable at given times of the day.

There is a lot more, so if you know nothing about any of this, this book is an excellent place to start. And if you do know something about chi kung, you still might find worthwhile information since Yang covers a lot of bases in some detail.

The next section is on the basic chi kung of seated meditation. Yang lays out the groundwork and methodology to be followed, and he enumerates what he calls the "mechanics of meditation," which consist of fourteen rules. Common problems a novice meditator might experience are covered next, then it's on to a description of the Grand Circulation, in which the chi is consciously circulated not just through the Small Circulation, but through the entire meridian system. At this point, Yang describes a set of seated chi kung that incorporates arm movement to teach the meditator to sense and willfully manipulate the chi. This material also is primarily for those who have no sensation of or control over their chi.

Chapter four covers chi kung and health, and it is principally concerned with TCM and its history, methodology, and effects. Massage and acupressure techniques are included.

The final chapter is on martial arts applications, but Yang doesn't take up space here with a lot of photos and descriptions of specific techniques being applied. Instead, he discusses the more targeted aspects of cavities and cavity strikes, sealing the breath, sealing the vein, and Iron Shirt and Golden Bell training. Techniques to develop the latter two are divulged, but this is not an instructional text, so the teaching material is slight. But Yang does provide a chart of the points that can affect the chi flow and the times of day they are most vulnerable.

Chi Kung contains many interesting ideas and their roles in the development and training of chi kung, TCM, and the martial arts. Intelligently written and highly informative, this was an important book of its day and remains so.

The Book of Internal Exercises

by Stephen T. Chang
with Richard C. Miller
(Strawberry Hill Press, 1978, 138 pages)

There are several books on the market that teach various sorts of internal exercises. Some are better than others, and this is one of the better ones. Unlike *The Chinese Way to a Long and Healthy Life* (see below), which demonstrates a number of chi kung exercises but contains little explanatory text aside from basic instruction, Stephen T. Chang's *The Book of Internal Exercises* is replete with information on chi and the meridian system and how they are affected by life and by particular exercises.

Author Chang was trained in Western medicine as well as in traditional Chinese medicine, and he is the author of a number of other books. Co-author Miller is an acknowledged master of Hatha Yoga, so both know what they are talking about when it comes to internal exercises. In fact, a number of the exercises in this book come from yoga rather than chi kung, per se. The three major chi kungs in the book are the Deer, the Crane, and the Turtle, each of which is thoroughly explicated in several forms. Next come a variety of yoga-like postures that work to strengthen or heal various parts of the body, including the eyes, nose, and sinuses in addition to the major organs.

A chapter on Taoist meditation and breathing comes next, which includes several stretching exercises that I used to be able to do when I was younger but that hurt me just to look at now. The book ends with a thorough chapter on circulating chi through the Microcosmic and Macrocosmic Orbits, here called the Small and Large Heavenly Cycles. If I have a quibble with anything in this book it is the authors' contention that circulating the chi through the Microcosmic and Macrocosmic Orbits should not be undertaken until the meridian system is free of blockages.

My problem here is that the chi always flows through the system, even if the flow is blocked and sluggish—otherwise, we'd be dead. Mindfully circulating the chi through the Orbits might require releasing some of the blockages first in addition to softening the body and loosening the joints, but in my experience, chi building and mobilizing exercises are progressive and cooperative endeavors. The more you unblock, soften, and loosen, the greater the flow and the greater the awareness of the flow. Becoming aware of the flow and mindfully, though gently, propelling the chi through the meridians further enables one to perform the unblocking, softening, and loosening. It's not that you create the system and then fill it up, but more that you open to the system and the awareness of the flow even as you increase the power of the flow and learn to manipulate it.

But this is a minor criticism of an otherwise excellent and informative book. Even if you do not undertake all the exercises contained in it, or undertake them in small increments, the book is well worth reading. It is well illustrated and, even better, still available. This is a valuable addition to any martial arts library and would serve the yoga community equally well.

The Chinese Way to a Long and Healthy Life
Diet, Exercise, Massage

Compiled and Edited by the People's Medical Publishing House
(Hippocrene Books, 1984, 304 pages)

The full authorship of this book is: By Various Chinese Experts and the Staff of the People's Medical Publishing House of Beijing, China. Obviously, this is a communal effort whose true author is the Chinese Government. Considering the negativity with which the Chinese Communist regime treated the various kung fu and chi kung arts, at least in the past, this might make some suspect the book for one reason or another. But it came out during a time when the Chinese government was reconsidering the benefits of these arts—to the government, of course—and had begun promoting wushu as an official state sport, so we might expect at least some validity in this book.

And that is the case. The expository material (background, philosophy, etc.) is minimal, and the majority of the pages are chock full of exercises, from stretching and limbering to massage to chi kung. The book even includes instructions for a simplified Taiji form. One caveat is that there is very little textual instruction, with the book relying on the illustrations to do that work. Could you learn these exercises from this book? Maybe, but it probably would take you a week of full-time effort to perform them all.

If you did, you'd be in really great condition, but most of us—in the West and most likely almost everywhere else in the world—don't have the time or inclination to devote that much effort toward the purely physical. I've found that the Taiji and chi kung forms and a few ancillary exercises I do are about all I have the time and energy for these days, though I used to do more in my younger years. The average reader might pick a few of the exercises to help with specific issues they have and leave the rest alone. Or they might try all of them a bit at a time to get a sense of the range they provide.

The final chapter is "Thirty Recipes for Medical Treatment and Health Care." The recipes range from juice and herbal drinks to soups to main courses. Some of them sound tasty—such as stewed chicken with maltose—while others are less so—bull's genitals cooked with Chinese wolfberry or pig's brain cooked with Chinese yam and Chinese wolfberry, for a couple of examples. Okay, I admit I'm not an adventurous eater.

I also admit that I bought this book in 1982, looked through it once, then put it on the shelf, where it's sat almost undisturbed since until I reread it for this review.

The Chinese Way to Family Health & Fitness: Wushu!

The People's Sports Publishing House
Material selected and translated by Timothy Tung
(Simon & Schuster/Mitchell Beazley Publishers, 1981, 144 pages)

The Chinese Way to Family Health & Fitness: Wushu! has almost as many chefs as it does dishes, and it offers a large menu. In basic content, if not in form, the book is similar to *The Chinese Way to a Long and Healthy Life* (reviewed above) by another Chinese Government department: the People's Medical Publishing House. Both are compendiums of kung fu, wushu, and chi kung exercises and other health techniques. This one begins with a two-page introduction by none other than Dame Margot Fonteyn, the prima ballerina assoluta of the English Royal Ballet, who writes briefly but knowingly on the basic parameters of the Chinese martial arts.

After that, it's nothing but workout after workout, arranged in three logical sections: external exercises, internal exercises, and exercises to prevent certain diseases. Each section opens with an introduction on the principles involved in its particular style of exercises, followed by several groups of exercises that often are linked together, sometimes in a form, sometimes in a routine. For example, the first cluster of exercises in the external exercise section is called "Silk Exercises." These consist of four sets, each with seven to ten individual exercises. This basic pattern holds true for every cluster of exercises, though the number of sets and individual activities varies.

The second cluster is interesting for a martial arts exercise book. Titled, "First-Year Exercises," it offers a number of exercise activities that a parent can do with an infant. Start 'em young. The other clusters are Playground Exercises, Farmer's Exercises, Coffee Break Exercises, and Animal Play. This last one displays exercises related to the tiger, bear, monkey, deer, and crane that go back to the dawn of Chinese martial arts. After showing each basic exercise, the chapter shows a large number of variations on each animal theme.

After an intro on principles, the section on internal exercises begins by demonstrating the twenty-eight-movement Taiji form created by the Chinese National Sports Committee. A short Taiji sword form follows, and the section winds up with several pages on push hands, here called "the Taiji Duet."

A great many of the exercises to prevent certain diseases are repeated from earlier sections, here given more of a medical slant. They are accompanied by other healthcare strategies, such as breathing, eye exercises, massage, and certain kinds of baths. The book closes with a table of the exercises previously described that lists their physical effects and points to remember.

Because most of the exercises in this book—excluding the Taiji forms—are simple movements that repeat, it should be fairly easy to learn whatever you want from this book. The exercise are succinctly but well explained, and they are accompanied by small but excellent drawings showing the body movements.

It's hard to criticize a book like this. The material is cogent, and the book is well done, informative within its scope, and illustrative of what it speak of. But it's also a sort of pick-and-choose sort of book. There's no way a person could do all these exercises daily and hold down a job—or maybe even sleep. But if you could, you'd be the fittest person around.

Self Healing
Chinese Exercises for Health and Longevity

By Erle Montaigue
(Boobook Publications, 1986, 80 pages.)

Self Healing, by Erle Montaigue, is a basic introduction to Chinese healing arts, including meditation, chi kung, Taiji, Bagua, massage, Taoist yoga, breathing strategies, and nutrition.

For those who don't know about Erle Montaigue, he was an Australian martial artist and teacher with expertise in all three of the major internal schools: Taiji, Bagua, and Xingyi. He learned these arts in China, even studying with Yang Sauchung, one of Yang Chengfu's sons. A prolific author, he wrote extensively on the internal martial arts, the death touch (dim-mak), and other aspects of Chinese healing arts. I count eighteen books that he authored and two that he coauthored, and he wrote many articles for martial arts publications. In addition, he was an early adopter of video to disseminate his teachings. He died of a heart attack in 2011 at age of sixty-two.

Montaigue covers his subjects roughly in the order listed in the first paragraph above. Chi kung is the most-covered subject in this slim volume, and he begins his discussion with a chapter on the history and basic philosophy of chi kung. This history—a glance at the principles of chi kung—is basically fine, but I take some exception with his definition of chi kung. The problem here is that he defines chi kung, which embodies an incredibly broad and diverse array of practices, simply as the one chi kung exercise known as Standing Post. There are many hundreds, if not thousands, of chi kung exercises, and though Standing Post is a powerful one in its own right, saying that it *is* chi kung is like saying a tree is a forest.

Okay, I'm being a little snarky here. Although Montaigue does offer this definition, he does show a couple of clusters of other chi kung exercises. And to his credit, he describes not only how to do them but what they are good for in terms of health and the meridian system.

From here, Montaigue goes on to describe Taiji, Bagua, Taoist yoga, massage, breathing techniques, and nutrition. Each of the first four contain several exercises or techniques, but the treatment of their subjects is superficial. The next chapter, on breathing strategies, is a bit more complex in terms of information, and it delineates several types of breathing techniques, describing both their function and purpose. The chapter on nutrition also is a little more involved, discussing nutrition in general before digressing on several types of foods that are beneficial or harmful.

I wanted to like this book more than I did. Montaigue was an acknowledged expert in the field of the internal martial arts, and I expected a lot more from the book, which turns out to be a rather superficial introduction to the subjects it covers. But at the same time, I expected to like this book less than I did. Its short length and superficiality left me begging for more depth and detail, but the truth is that there actually is a lot of worthwhile information in it—especially for beginners looking for a quick survey of traditional Chinese medicine and the internal martial arts.

One final criticism is that the writing, while readable, is somewhat choppy and sloppy. This might be due to the fact that the book is one of Montaigue's earliest. I haven't read his later works to see if his literary style improved over time. Perhaps later.

Prolonging Life
Ridding Illness without Medicine

by Yin Qianhe
(Pole Star Press & Joined in Harmony Press, 1961. *Brennan Translations*, 2015. 202 pages.)

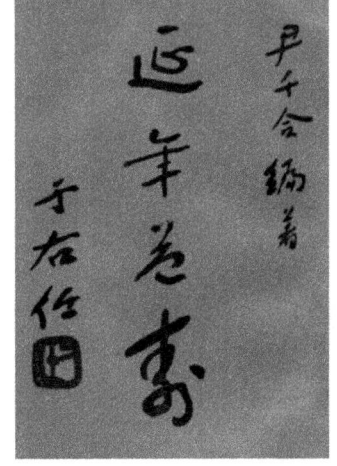

In *Prolonging Life: Ridding Illness without Medicine*, Yin Qianhe has assembled a thorough manual on health and self-healing based on traditional Chinese medicine. With the exception of a few chapters, this is not a book to be read for insights or understandings. Instead, it is a catalog of techniques and methods to combat illness, whether transitory or chronic. The opening sentence of the book says it all:

> My aim with this book is a hope that you will keep fit by way of internal exercises, using psychology, physiology, and natural principles to treat and cure illness, as well as [by] methods of first aid, and the expressing of human willpower, to dispel illness invisibly.

The emphasis here is, first, on prevention of illness and, second, on curing it. Yin begins the treatise with several introductory sections that lay out his basic background in the martial arts and meditation and how those led him to a deeper understanding of health and well-being. The purpose of his book, he writes, is to share his knowledge for the benefit of his fellow human beings.

You could call this a mid-20th century Chinese version of contemporary American self-help and self-healing literature.

Over the course of twenty-nine chapters, each containing several sections, Yin discusses a great number of health-related exercises, practices, and dietary suggestions. The first three chapters are those that most probably would interest the general reader. In chapter one, he defines the basic parameters of internal energy and discusses the idea of cultivating it through specific exercises and practices. Along the way, he gives reasons to take up these exercises and practices as well as warning against certain pitfalls. Chapter two, while still remaining philosophical, discusses health and illness in more specific terms, still with a concentration on internal energy. Chapter three comprises four somewhat lengthy passages from previous Chinese elixirist literature, all of which are intrinsically interesting.

The focus of chapters four and five is massage techniques. The reason to use each technique is explained, and the descriptions of the technique's methods are adequate, but each one is accompanied by only a single photo of poor quality. Meditation is the subject of chapter six. Three methods are discussed—standing, sitting, and lying—and each has a photo. This is a pretty basic gloss of a very deep subject.

Chi kung takes up chapter seven, and in it, Yin gives a general explanation of chi kung exercises as well as discussions of the psychology of chi kung and breathing techniques, including abdominal breathing. Chapter eight goes back to the subject of massage, and chapter nine is a brief discussion of how to practice chi kung. I'd have put chapter eight alongside chapter six, which would have combined all the massage material in one section and all the chi kung material in another, instead of leap-frogging back and forth between them, which was confusing.

Chapter ten, which contains various saying from authors other than Yin about health and nourishing life and internal energy, also will interest the general reader.

With the exception of the final chapter, the entire remainder of the book—about 75 percent of the total—is given over to discussions of a vast number of illnesses and conditions, ranging from digestive issues to problems of the eyes, ears, nose, and throat, to athlete's foot and acne, and on and on. Each is furnished with a set of cures or palliatives, though some are old-fashioned in the light of modern medicines.

I'd call this a sort of home-cure manual since none of the cures involve doctors, and all of them can be accomplished through physical actions, such as exercise or the spreading of balms, or through dietary supplements that one can make at home if you have access to the right ingredients. That might be difficult, since you'd have to have access to a Chinese herbalist to concoct some of these remedies. Also, quite a few of these cures do not sound palatable, and the reader should take all of them with a proverbial grain of salt—or maybe the real thing. Yin also discusses a vast range of food stuffs and delineates their benefits and side effects.

In the final chapter, titled, "Some Further Thoughts," Yin presents a number of maxims on life in general and on ethics and moral purpose more specifically, again by other authors. This chapter also would be of interest to the general reader.

As I implied earlier, *Prolonging Life* is not a book to be read through in its entirety, though a number of chapters do lend themselves to that purpose. For the most part, it would primarily appeal either to readers who already have an interest in self-help literature and self-healing techniques or to those who want to research cures for practical reasons.

Those interested in Yin Quianhe's other writings on Taiji can find reviews of those in this volume and in Volumes III, IV, and VII of this series.

The Art of Breathing
Thirty Simple Exercises for Improving Your Performance and Well-being

by Nancy Zi
(Bantam Books, 1986, 160 pages)

As experienced Taiji players know, Taiji isn't just waving your arms around in the air, even if it seems like that to onlookers not versed in the art. Rather, we are trying to fill our bodies and limbs with chi and learning how to manipulate that energy within us—and sometimes outside of us. But even if all living things embody chi, awareness of this energy and the means to amplify and manipulate it don't just happen automatically.

The word chi has alternate meanings in Chinese, but it is generally linked both to internal energy and to air and respiration. There's a good reason for that. Respiration is the engine that creates chi and propels it through the body. (I discuss the mechanisms of that in my own book, *The Wellspring: An Inquiry into the Nature of Chi*, for those who are curious.) Proper breathing technique is as essential to the correct performance of Taiji as are correct body alignments, relaxation, and a flexible waist. Unfortunately, most books on Taiji do not adequately discuss breathing, concentrating instead on the physical movements and implying that the chi flows naturally from the postures.

Not so. Correct postures will facilitate and direct chi flow, but they are more akin to positioning a water pipe so that water is able to flow freely through it. Postures, in and of themselves, do not generate chi or cause it to flow. Chi is created in the tantien, often described as a point a couple of inches below and behind the navel, but this is misleading, too. Chi is created in the mass of intestines housed in the belly, and this mass is the real tantien. This mass produces chi as a direct result of mechanical stimulation, which is dramatically heightened by abdominal breathing.

Taiji books that do talk about breathing all say the same thing: Breathe abdominally. This means using a downward expansion and upward contraction of the diaphragm to pull air into the lungs and expel it again, rather than an outward and inward movement of the muscles of the chest wall. The downward expansion is what causes the mechanical stimulation of the intestines and the resulting amplification of chi. Some of these books also discuss the differences between what is called "natural abdominal breathing" and its alternative, "reverse abdominal breathing." I don't want to go into that here, because that's a whole other discussion not specifically related to the content of Nancy Zi's *The Art of Breathing*.

The key is that the techniques of abdominal breathing are critical to the generation of chi. Breathing abdominally is the only way to amplify and more strongly propel chi through the body. Zi is a classical singer, and as many readers know, good singing comes from the belly, not the chest, and thus employs abdominal breathing. Zi's other interest is chi kung, though her book is addressed primarily to singers. But while the book does not discuss Taiji, per se, the information is highly relevant to the art. In the book, Zi combines her knowledge of the two disciplines of singing and chi kung to deliver not just a deep understanding of the physiology of breathing, but some of the most sound information and advice available on this critical aspect of the internal martial arts. This advice includes not just the concept and methodology of abdominal breathing, but also practical exercises to enhance its application and effects. Many of them are chi kung exercises designed to amplify the chi and open up the body to allow the chi to flow more fully.

It would be pointless here to try to go into the specific content of the book. I'll let Zi do that for herself. But I will say that this is a well-written and engaging textbook on abdominal breathing and its techniques. It is adequately illustrated in terms of quantity, very well in terms of quality. If you haven't learned abdominal breathing and applied it to your Taiji, you're missing out. Zi's book can help you overcome this deficit and make your Taiji more empowering, no matter what your purpose in practicing. A nuts-'n-bolts book, *The Art of Breathing* just might be essential to your Taiji training.

The Chi Revolution
Harness the Healing Power of Your Life Force

by Bruce Frantzis
(Thorsons, 2003, 292 pages)

Bruce Frantzis has become pretty well known since I first saw articles he wrote for *Tai Chi Magazine* back in the 1980s. These days, he's one of the more successful of the crop of American Taiji players who've risen to the top of their game during the past couple of decades. He's also a fairly prolific writer on Taiji, chi kung, Bagua, and Xingyi, with a double-handful of books to his credit, some of which are fairly hefty tomes.

In the dedication to *The Chi Revolution: Harness the Healing Power of Your Life Force*, Frantzis writes:

> This book is the culmination of all the knowledge of chi I have acquired in over forty years as a martial artist, chi master, Taoist priest and energetic healer.

Perhaps, though as we all know, words simply can't say everything, and Taiji and chi kung are pretty deep subjects. Nonetheless, Frantzis has produced in this book a fairly interesting survey that defines chi, both microcosmically and macrocosmically, encourages the reader to take up chi-building and -developing exercises, and gives practical examples to accomplish that.

I have to admit that I'm not a fan of self-help and self-realization books—the sort of book that combines a rather amorphous sense that we, too, are gods, with the idea that, despite our godhood, we need the author's help to give our lives meaning or to fulfill our destinies. It's not that I don't believe that we, as individuals, can't do something to better ourselves. I do. Heck, I've been practicing Taiji for more than forty years, so I must think we can do something to make ourselves more whole. It's just that too many of these books are page after page of "positive thinking" that all too often seems more like wishful thinking.

The Chi Revolution dips a little too deeply into this territory for my taste, but Frantzis is a good enough writer that he can maintain an extended narrative such as this, and he drops enough solid information here and there to keep it real and interesting for the most part. Perhaps one of the more significant aspects is that he draws a direct link between discomforts, faults, and deficiencies that are physical and those that are mental, emotional, and spiritual. It's not a new idea, but Frantzis provides practical ways to help integrate the body, mind, and spirit through specific chi-building and developing exercises. These exercises comprise roughly the second half of the book.

Even though the book contains some instructional material, I think it's best defined as an extended meditation on chi arts and what they mean on a larger scale as well as for individuals. All-in-all, this book is for the beginner or intermediate student, and I can't say I really learned anything from it. But it was a nice enough read, and sometimes it's reinforcing to hear, once more, how things work and why we should try to make them work better.

The Tao of Health and Longevity

by Da Liu
(Schocken Books, 1978, 178 pages)

Da Liu might be largely forgotten now, but he should be recognized as an early disseminator of Taiji in America—at about the same time that Sophia Delza, Edward Maisel, and Robert W. Smith also were introducing the art to Westerners. In his several books, Liu tends to treat the health, philosophical, and developmental aspects of Taiji rather than the martial, and *The Tao of Health and Longevity* is no exception. He acknowledges Taiji's martial superiority, but he also points out that as people age, their interests and focus changes from external conflict to the search for inner peace. Taiji, he maintains, is a sure road to the latter, as long as one keeps one's feet surely on the path.

Liu sometimes lets his enthusiasm for actual physical longevity get in the way of his reason. Throughout history, there have been numerous claims of human longevity exceeding 130 years, and Liu cites three: "the remarkable Taoist master Li Ch'ing Yuen, who lived to be 250 years old"; Shirali Mislimov (Muslimov), who was reputedly 170 at the time of his death; and American Charlie Smith, who was 137. I don't know anything about Li, but Mislimov's self-reported date of birth is disputed, and various public records indicate that Smith was really 105 at the time of his death. The longest-lived person officially on record was Frenchwoman Jeanne Calment, who died at 122.

I think it is a mistake to equate longevity with length of life rather than with quality of life. In his book, *Tai Chi Dynamics*, Robert Chuckrow displays a list of prominent Taiji masters and their ages at death. His chart dramatically shows that Taiji does not naturally or automatically impart extremely long life. Only two of the masters listed exceeded one hundred years of age, and a surprising number didn't even reach sixty.

So rather than thinking of longevity as absolute length of life, I tend to consider it to be the staving off of creeping decrepitude for as long as one is able. For Calment, that was a really long time, while for others, it is shorter. The point is to retain health, flexibility, and mobility during the course of one's life, however long it might last. Possibly these will impart a longer lifespan since a healthy lifestyle tends not to damage one's body, but certainly they will make what lifespan we do have more interesting and useful as well as tolerable. Quality of life rather than length is the real point of Liu's book, and he rightly attributes an improved quality of life to Taiji.

From his discussion on longevity, Liu goes into a history of Chinese philosophy and religion, including a substantial section on Taoism and another on Confucianism. The chapter after that covers the various physiological structures directly affected by Taiji—the central nervous system, digestive system, respiratory system, circulatory system, and endocrine system—and along the way, he explains the concept of chi.

Breathing occupies an entire chapter, and Liu gives a few breathing exercises—without illustrations—both to explain his concepts and to give the reader practical guides to follow. Next comes the form instruction section for a version of Yang style. I didn't analyze the form to see if it is a standard Yang style, but it numbers ninety-three movements rather than the usual 108. The text is fairly explanatory and the photos are clear but without directional arrows or charts of foot-stepping patterns. Ultimately, this is no better and no worse than the average for this type of material.

A handful of chi kung movements occupy the next chapter, but there are few photos or illustrations. The chapter after deals with aspects of health not directly related to Taiji or chi kung, such as diet, clothing, and shelter, and the effects of various movements people perform daily, such as walking, sitting, and sleeping.

Massage and acupressure are the subjects of the next chapter, which discusses how one can perform these on oneself to cure various minor ailments such as headache, sore throat, and stomach ache. No photos or illustrations go with these descriptions. Food occupies the next chapter, and Liu details several recipes for healthful and curative foods.

"The Relationship Between Man and Woman" is the title of the final chapter. Taoist sex practices are not often dealt with in Taiji literature, and while this chapter can't be taken as the *Kama Sutra* of Taiji, at least Liu addresses the subject.

This may not be one of the best beginner's books on Taiji, but it has a fair amount of information for beginners, especially those more interested in Taiji as an exercise and life enhancer rather than as a martial art. And a lot of that information would be of use even to the martially oriented.

Kunwu Sword Neigong

By Jiang Rongqiao
(Originally published 1930. *Brennan Translations*, 2020, 40 pages)

Don't be fooled by the word, "sword," in the title. Most of the book features a nei kung (internal chi kung) designed to prepare one's body to wield a sword through bending, twisting, stretching, and strengthening of the arms and wrists. It does not feature any swordplay.

Jiang Rongqiao (1891-1974) was a famous internal stylist in his day, known, as was Sun Lutang, for creating a synthesis of Taiji, Bagua, and Xingyi: Taiji Zhang Quan (Taiji Palm and Fist), that eventually morphed into Jiang Style Baguazhang.[1] Jiang's book, *Bagua Practice Methods*, was the first book on Bagua to be published after the 1949 revolution, and it greatly enhanced his reputation. Unfortunately, he was blinded in an accident, and his adopted daughter, Zou Shuxian, assisted him in writing the Bagua book as well as being a disciple. He authored and co-authored a number of books, some of which are reviewed in other volumes of this series.

The Kunwu sword form was a fairly famous style that may have had its mythic origin in a sword called Kunwu that was given to the legendary Yellow Emperor, Huang Ti, by Juitian Xuannü, the Chinese goddess of war, sex, and longevity, to assist him in defeating a rival leader named Chiyou. Supposedly, Kunwu was capable of slaying gods and demons and was able to repel evil magic.[2,3]

Whatever the case might be, in this book, Jiang is interested in preparing you to perform the Kunwu Sword form. He leads off with this:

> We can consider the practice of Qingping Sword and Kunwu Sword to be "sword arts" or "sword knowledge," but it is in either case external training. Therefore it is necessary to engage in internal training [nei gong] to supplement it, for the internal and external must both be cultivated, and then your study of the sword will be properly enriched.

The set consists of thirty-six movements.

> The first twenty-seven movements brighten the eyes, open the ears, improve the breathing of the lungs, and benefit the vital organs and the brain. The purpose of the internal training is to provide a stairway into the learning of the sword art. The final nine postures are the basics in a study of the sword, and yet are still a phase of internal training. To your hands, feet, and hips, these exercises will bring countless benefits and not one harm.

Then Jiang moves straight into the exercises. As noted above, most of the exercises consist of simple bending, stretching, and twisting accompanied by regulated breathing, though a couple are more strenuous, such as doing Snake Slithers Down and touching your forehead to the floor.

The instructions indicate that the exercises move from one to the next, but as discreet exercises rather than as a flow, as with a Taiji form. All of these exercises seem to be basic chi kung until, as the author states, number twenty-eight. From there to the end, the exercises are more specifically related to the sword, and several of them deal with training rapid footwork.

There are literally thousands of chi kung exercises out there in the world. What makes these special is that they are designed specifically to prepare the sword-wielder to more thoroughly control his weapon, and it would probably be beneficial for practitioners of any Chinese sword form.

Notes

1 "Jiang Rong Qiao." *Wikipedia*, https://en.wikipedia.org/wiki/Jiang_Rong_Qiao
2 "List of Mythological Objects." *Wikipedia*, https://en.wikipedia.org/wiki/List_of_mythological_objects
3 "Jian." *Wikipedia*, https://en.wikipedia.org/wiki/Jian

An Authentic Depiction of Damo's Yijinjing

By Jin Ti'an
(Originally published 1936. *Brennan Translations*, 2020, 18 pages)

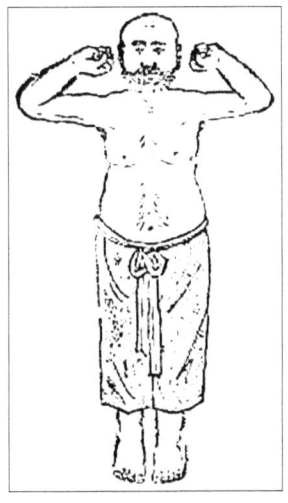

There are a lot of chi kung exercises out there in the world, both external (wai kung) and internal (nei kung), but they all owe a great debt to their great-great-many-times-great-grandfather: Damo's Yijinjing, better known in English as the Sinew Change Classic.

Anyone who has read much about the martial arts should know the story of Damo—more properly, Bodhidharma—traveling from India to the Shaolin Monastery in China to disseminate Buddhist philosophy. Finding the monks at Shaolin weak and their meditations ineffectual, he taught them the Sinew Changes and Eighteen Luohan Hands—both being sets of exercises designed to strengthen and invigorate the practitioner and which, over time, were transformed by the monks into the many forms of Shaolin kung fu.

There are a number of different interpretations of the Sinew Change exercises, and Jin treats us to a sequence of twelve exercises. Each is described in text and a single adequate line drawing. They are all pretty easy to do, but to get real benefits, you have to exert some strength since these are basic wai kung.

These days, chi kung—both external and internal—have been developed to reasonably high degrees of sophistication for health and martial usage, so the Sinew Change seems rather primitive by comparison. But sometimes basic is best, and bells-and-whistles only add dross. Take your pick of chi kung, but be aware that the exercises featured in the book are geared more for the external stylist.

A Handbook for Twelve-Posture Yijinjing

A Handbook for Twenty-Four-Posture Yijinjing

By Wang Huaiqi
(Both originally published by Merchant Publishing House, 1917. *Brennan Translations*, 2017, 38/34 pages)

Although author Wang Huaiqi calls both of these sets of exercises "Yijinjing," neither is the same as the Yijinjing covered by Jin Ti'an in his *An Authentic Depiction of Damo's Yijinjing*, reviewed above. It also should be clear that the chi kung offered by this book are of the external sort, and perhaps not as simple as the Damo version, although the author says that Damo created this sequence, too. He writes:

> It seems to me that Baduanjin [the Eight Pieces of Brocade] brings results very quickly because its postures and movements are all simple. But for this exercise, although the postures are simple, the movements are more complex, therefore one who has not practiced any other foundational exercises might find this material somewhat difficult.

We'll cover *A Handbook for Twelve-Posture Yijinjing* first. Wang begins with a brief overview that leads into a number of precepts and principles of the practice, and they're all pretty good points to keep in mind no matter what you're doing. He then digresses on exercising various specific parts of the body: fingers, eyes, legs, hands, feet, and the limbs.

Next he presents six pages of old illustrations showing Damo's "original set" before moving on to the instruction section, which takes up most of the book. All the exercises shown seem to combine calisthenics, bending, and stretching with breathing patterns. Each is treated to a textual description that is accompanied by a photo. Each photo usually has Wang and another young man in two poses, one that moves to the other—this is in lieu of arrows showing the direction of movement. In some ways, this method might be more edifying than arrows. The exercises are definitely external, but they also look effective. Indeed, Wang looks pretty fit in his cover photo.

To be clear, the exercises in *A Handbook for Twenty-Four Posture Yijinjing* are similar to those in the *Twelve-Posture* book but do not replicate them. Instead, this is a different sequence that seems a little more strenuous than the Twelve-Posture set. As with the previous book, there are only a couple of pages of background and philosophy, and the majority of the pages are devoted to the instruction section.

These are good exercises, but as I discovered long ago, one cannot do every chi kung or kung fu form. One has to pick and choose. I tend to opt for internal chi kung, but for those who prefer the external sort, these sets should give you a workout.

Scientific Martial Arts

By Wu Zhiqing
(Originally published as *Using Martial Arts to Make China's New Calisthenics*, 1919/1920. Serialized in *Martial Arts Magazine* as *Applying Science to Martial Arts*, 1921. Brennan Translations, 2019, 72 pages)

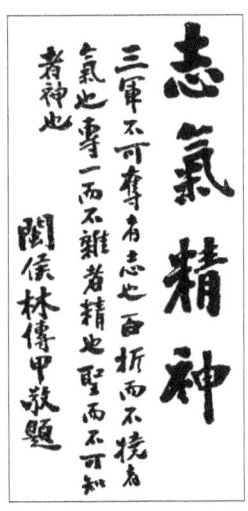

Despite the title, this isn't a martial arts instruction manual. Instead, it is a compendium of martial arts exercises, mostly external chi kung, gathered from various sources. The author writes:

> For this book, I have selected from the best exercises from various styles of Chinese martial arts and adjusted the movement in accordance with principles of physiology, psychology, and pedagogy. I would not dare claim that these exercises are perfect, but they they are all on the side of the realistic rather than the absurd, which is why I have call the book *Scientific Martial Arts*.

The book leads with, as is often the case with Chinese martial arts manuals, a number of prefaces. These are by Shen Enfu, Lin Chuanjia, Wie Qianggong, Tang Xinyu, and Chi Juezai. All extol the virtues of physical fitness and the martial arts, both for personal health and well-being and for national well-being. They all also speak to the author's expertise.

Wu's own introduction is much the same, at least regarding the need for personal and national health. He, like a lot of martial arts authors, evinces a humble attitude about his own skills, abilities, and knowledge.

The first matter he addresses is the relationship between martial arts and physiology, psychology, and pedagogy. His explanations don't go far, but it is obvious he is more interested in delivering the instructional material than he is in expounding on history, purposes, philosophy, methodology, and so forth of the material he is teaching.

Wu describes seven separate exercise sets, each set made up of several movements (usually eight to ten, but occasionally more) done as a sequence—sort of like mini-forms. They are performed on both sides of the body. The sets are:

1) An Exercise for the Four Limbs
2) An Exercise of Realigning
3) An Exercise for the Upper Body
4) An Exercise for the Waist and Hips
5) An Exercise for Quickness
6) An Exercise for Slowness
7) A Breathing Exercise

Each of these has explanations of the movements, photos, and digressions regarding the three important aspects of the exercise that Wu has already mentioned: the physiological, psychological, and pedagogical. The photos aren't so good, but you can tell what's going on.

This ends the book proper, but several chapters remain. The first is the preface to the reprinted edition. The second is an article reprinted from the *Shanghai Evening News* about a banquet hosted by Wu Zhiqing. The purpose of the banquet, which included Anglo as well as Chinese luminaries, was a celebration of physical education. This is followed by a couple of reviews of the event, also from the *Shanghai Evening News*.

Next come two reports on the Chinese Martial Arts Exhibition, which was part of the 5th Far Eastern Championship Games of June 1921. These chapters provide an interesting glimpse into the Chinese martial arts world in the early years of the Republican Era. The book closes with a postscript by Wu further encouraging the reader to practice the martial arts.

These seem to be good exercises, but since they involve sequences of movement, they are probably a little more difficult to learn than are repetitive-type chi kung exercises. And they are all of the external sort and so are more suitable for external stylists rather than internal stylists.

Fitness Techniques on a Bed

Scientific Baduanjin

By Yin Qianhe
(Originally published 1958. *Brennan Translations*, 2013, 36 pages)

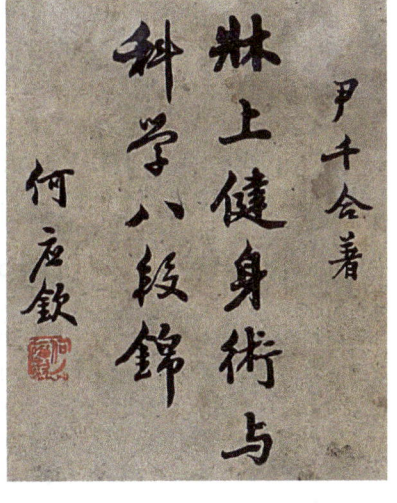

No, this is not a salacious book. The "bed" referred to in the first title is actually nothing more than an exercise mat on the floor, although the author, Yin Qianhe, encourages the reader to practice them on the bed before sleep and upon waking.

I can't tell you much about Yin Qianhe except to say that he fought against the Japanese during the Sino-Japanese War. After the Communist takeover, he fled to Taiwan, where he became a schoolteacher. And he continued his study of the martial arts with the many other expert martial artists who, like him, had fled Mainland China. Translator Paul Brennan has posted five books by him on *Brennan Translations*, and I've reviewed all of them in this series, plus one translation by another individual.

Between them, the two manuals contained in this volume depict two external chi kung forms (wai kung) and one internal chi kung (nei kung). They are led off by two prefaces—by Shen Honglie and Chen Panling—and a third by the author. The first two are basically accolades and pep talks. Yin's preface tells how he was ill as a youth and that his health improved to a high level thanks to his practice of the martial arts.

The main text leads off with general comments by the author. Regarding the contents of the book, the two most important are:

> The movements in this book are very mild, easy, and scientific. I have considered the old as a means to prepare the new, so these exercises can be practiced by both male and female, young and old, and are especially suitable for the old and weak.

And:

> This book conforms to the principles of physiology and anatomy. Practicing the material can not only promote health, it can also prevent and treat illness.

The purpose of the bed exercises is to make the ill and weak well and stronger and capable of undertaking the more strenuous Baduanjin sets in the second book.

A list of things that must be understood comes next:

1) When practicing, you should calm your mind and pacify your energy, eliminating desirous thoughts.
2) You should be persevering and should not expect quick results.
3) You should look upon the exercise as being for health and so should not use excessive effort.
4) The movement should be slow, and the breathing should be deep, long, and even.
5) The postures should be correct, and the actions must be done appropriately.
6) Practice every morning, going through the exercises at least twice, depending on your level of strength.
7) Before practicing, drink a bowl of boiled water with some added salt to flush your stomach and intestines.
8) In the beginning, your muscles will probably experience some aching, but you should persist and believe in the exercises.

He then lists a number of benefits:

1) They do not take up much time or require special facilities, they can be practiced anytime and anywhere.
2) They are easy to learn and easy to practice, not requiring a teacher, thereby granting the effect of twice the result for half the effort.
3) They smooth your digestive organs, assisting digestion and increasing appetite.
4) They harmonize blood and energy, invigorating your brain and refreshing your spirit.
5) They diminish inflammation and regenerate tissue, increasing the power of your immune system, reducing the risk of sudden infections.
6) They take into account both inside and out, strengthening both stomach and lungs, and can uniformly develop your whole body.
7) They increase your energy and strengthen your physique, promoting both health and beauty.
8) They prevent disease and bring longevity, giving you happiness for your whole life.

Instruction in the bed techniques comes next. There are eight exercises, all of which are stretching combined with mild calisthenics, all done while either sitting or prone. As the author promises, they are not strenuous, so those who have been ill or who are weak for one reason or another can do them and reap benefits.

Scientific Baduanjin follows. This presents a version of the Eight Pieces of Brocade, which seems to be performed differently by just about everybody who practices it. Yin's version is somewhat more strenuous than most and includes an exercise akin to Taiji's Snake Slithers Down.

The final set of exercises is Self-Revitalizing Baduanjin, which also consists of eight exercises. Unlike the previous two sets, which are wai kung, this set is a nei kung whose purpose is to vitalize the internal energy.

As Yin claims, these exercises are indeed simple to learn and perform—except, perhaps, for the movement that resembles Snake

Slithers Down. But for Taiji practitioners, even this one shouldn't be too difficult, despite the fact that the photos are really poor.

The Luohan Exercises

By Xu Longhou
(Originally published within *Collected Materials on Physical Education*, 1924. Brennan Translations, 2021, 84 pages)

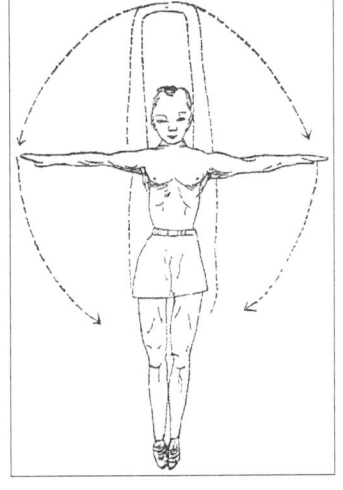

Xu Longhou, also known as Xu Yusheng, was a disciple of the Yang family's first three generations of exponents. Although he was not a formal disciple of Yang Shouhou, he learned from him and was considered to be one of the best exponents of Shouhou's fast, small-frame form. This is the same form that eventually morphed into Wu Family Taiji, and more specifically, the Wu Style fast form.[1,2]

However, *The Luohan Exercises* by Xu Longhou is not a Taiji book but one that elucidates and demonstrates one version of the 18 Luohan Hands exercises supposedly taught to the monks at the Shaolin Temple by Bodhidharma (Damo). He taught them to improved their health and concentration, and those exercises, combined with his Eight Pieces of Brocade wai kung, were eventually developed by the monks into Shaolin kung fu.

The Luohan Exercises is a straightforward and rather thorough rendition of 18 Luohan Hands. It begins with a preface that gives general comments on the need for exercise and the benefits of 18 Luohan Hands. Next comes a list of important points, precepts, and methodology.

The history of 18 Luohan Hands follows, but it begins with comments on the general character of the art before dealing with any history. And the history it deals with is not the one usually told. In this version, Bodhidharma is not in evidence. Instead, the history deals more with the subsequent dissemination of the art beyond the Shaolin Temple walls, mostly through the efforts of a Taoist named Shengxiao.

A "Song of the Exercises" follows, poetically instructing the reader in the way to achieve success through practicing the 18 Luohan Exercises. After that comes the form instruction section, which occupies the remainder of the book.

To be clear, each of these exercises is not a matter of doing repetitions of simple body movements. Each one of them comprises several movements, which are described in the text and in several adequate line drawings. Most of these drawings were done by the same artist, but scattered here and there are some that are not stylistically the same. This isn't a detriment, and I only note it because it's curious.

Can you learn these exercises from this book? Yes, and they'd probably get you into shape pretty quickly. But for the internal martial artists, it's important to remember that these are most definitely wai kung, or external chi kung, that probably aren't as appropriate for internal stylists as are nei kung, or internal chi kung.

See the next two reviews for other books on the Luohan Exercises, starting with one by the Taoist Shengxiao.

Notes
1 "Yang Shou-hou." *Wikipedia*, https://en.wikipedia.org/wiki/Yang_Shao-hou
2 "Wu Style Tai Fast Form." *Wikipedia*, https://en.wikipedia.org/wiki/Wu_Style_Tai_Chi_Fast_Form

See also
"Luohan Quan." *Wikipedia*, https://en.wikipedia.org/wiki/Luohan_quan

Wisdom of the Luohans of the Western Regions

By the Taoist Shengxiao
Originally from *Authentic Teachings of Shaolin*, c. 1800. Brennan Translations, 2021, 70 pages)

This no-frills and rather old manual on the Eight Luohan Hands is almost all form instruction—and pretty good instruction, at that. The form instruction begins without preamble. Each of the eighteen exercises is broken into two to four parts for easy assimilation. The textual instructions are good, and the drawings, although in an archaic style, manage to convey the movements more accurately than do most old drawings of chi kung or martial arts movements. As a note, this is one vigorous workout more suited to the younger than the older practitioner.

What little expository material there is appears following the form instruction section, beginning with an internal anatomy chart. This drawing—or others very similar to it—has appeared in other Taiji and chi kung books, and all the parts are labeled in Chinese. Translator Paul Brennan gives a list in English alongside the Chinese characters, but he doesn't number anything, so you'll have to compare the characters in the list with the characters on the drawing to suss out what's what.

The book closes with several paragraphs and poems that further impart information about the exercises and what to pay attention to while practicing.

Despite the paucity of ancillary text, this is an excellent manual that really could teach you how to perform this set of Luohan exercises. For other books on the same Luohan set, see both the previous and the next review.)

The Luohan Exercises

By Huang Hanxun
(Originally published 1958. *Brennan Translations*, 2021, 88 pages)

The expository material in this manual, as with the one on the Luohan exercises reviewed above, is basically nil. There is a foreword by Huang Jinhong and another by the author, but neither does much more than state the provenance of the form. This is followed by a reproduction of the pages of an older Luohan manual by Fan Xudong that provided the basis of the current manual.

Then it's on to the form instruction section. The textual instructions are about on par with those of the Daoist Shengxiao's book, but instead of quaint drawings, this one contains photos of a man performing the movements. The photos aren't great, but they are adequate and probably provide a somewhat better template to follow than the old drawings do. The form instruction section ends the book.

This might be a bare-bones manual, but it's form instruction section would be easy to follow, especially if one were to pay heed to both books.

An Authentic Depiction of Yue Fei's Baduanjin

By Jin Ti'an
(Originally published 1936. Brennan Translations, 2020, 32 pages)

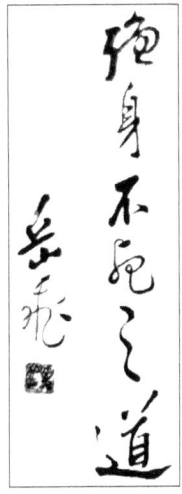

With this manual, we have yet another version of Baduanjin, or, the Eight Pieces of Brocade chi kung exercises. This set supposedly originated with Yue Fei, the famous Chinese general and martial artist whose legacy includes the creation of, or serious contribution to, several martial arts, including Xingyi, Bafan, and Praying Mantis. Author Jin Ti'an states that the book under consideration began as a handwritten manuscript by his boyhood teacher, a man named Gui, to which Jin added his own commentary.

Baduanjin essentially are a wai kung style of chi kung, meaning that they are external in nature and deal primarily with the body, as opposed to nei kung, which are chi kung that invigorate the chi system. Many wai kung, however, do work with chi, but only in localized areas instead of throughout the entire body.

Everybody who teaches the Eight Pieces of Brocade seems to do it differently, though there always are some similar movements. Pick this on, pick that one…. It doesn't seem to matter as long as you *do* something. This book's version is as good as another, I suppose, though I do like a couple of other versions better.

The Warrior Athlete
Body, Mind, Spirit

By Dan Millman
(Stillpoint Publishing, 1979, 172 pages)

Dan Millman is a notable gymnast, coach, and author of twenty books that combine advice and methods of athletic training with aspects of personal development. While all this doesn't seem very martial arts-oriented, clearly there are crossovers between gymnastics and the martial arts, and if the martial arts aren't methods of self-development, I guess I don't know the meaning of the term.

Millman is no tyro. As a high school gymnast, he won the United States Gymnastic Federation national title on the trampoline, and as a freshman at UC Berkeley, he won the 1964 Trampoline World Championships, All-America honors, and a NCAA championship in vaulting. Two years later, he won the USGF championship in floor exercises and represented the U.S. in the Maccabiah Games, where he won four Gold Medals in gymnastics.

Later that same year, he was in a motorcycle accident that shattered his right femur. Following extensive surgery and rehabilitation, he returned to gymnastics as co-captain of the Berkeley team, which won the 1968 NCAA Gymnastic Championships. His performance on the high bar earned him a best-ever routine with a perfect landing, cinching the title. He graduated with a degree in psychology. Gymnastics and psychology. Hmm. A decidedly powerful pair when linked together, and Millman does a fine job of linking.

Following graduation, he served as director of gymnastics for Stanford University, where he coached Olympian Steve Hug. During that time, he also trained in Aikido, eventually earning a black belt, and he also studied Taiji and other martial arts. His work is generally considered to be connected to the human potential movement.[1] *The Warrior Athlete* is Millman's third book, right after his most famous work, *The Way of the Peaceful Warrior*, which was made into a film of the same name.[1]

I would characterize *The Warrior Athlete* as an extended coaching session that focuses not on athletics, per se, but on the qualities that underlie athletic achievement, no matter what sport or activity one engages in. He's not going to tell you how to perform a backflip, but he will help you understand what needs to happen before and during athletic endeavor and, especially, what's going on inside the athlete. In this respect, nearly all of the lessons of this book can apply to the study and learning of any martial art, but particularly Taiji and Aikido since Millman's main focus is on focus and smooth, natural actions.

Millman begins with an introduction on the natural athlete in action, who he describes, as would Taiji folks, as having an infant's softness, flexibility, and drive to achieve the next wobbly step. Then he carries this concept into daily life, where athletic training suffuses every aspect of the athlete's life. (Millman's book is about athletics, but feel free to substitute "martial artist" for "athlete" at any time.) Here is where focus becomes important, for one can focus on the near and discernible or on the distant and challenging. It all depends, he says, on what you want to get out of your endeavor. Those who just want to remain reasonably fit have a different focus from the athlete—amateur or professional—who must strive to reach deeper levels of achievement and comprehension. And beyond that are the masters—those who have gone far enough that achievement and comprehension become one.

Part one of the book covers what Millman calls, "The Map." Essentially, this is a game plan for your future athletic achievement—a setting of goals and planning practical ways to reach them. First, obviously, must come an understanding of the rules of the game. Here, the main rules come from the lessons of nature, and they read like an explanation of Taiji principles: nonresistance, accommodation, balance, and natural order. He explains each at length, and each has a secondary explanation that takes in the psychophysical applications, or, the way each can be applied to one's life.

The next chapter covers awareness, which allows one to open to nature's lessons. In this context, the author discusses using self-awareness to discover one's own errors, which is prerequisite to correcting them. Thus, he says, awareness isn't always an easy thing to deal with, but it is a necessary one. This leads to a section on whole-body awareness, which isn't just finding one's own physical errors but is intimately bound up with one's awareness of mental and emotional states. Correcting these, Millman says, is critical to correcting and opening the physical state. He spends some space detailing these issues and illustrates them with several anecdotes and pithy statements, such as:

> Teachers who understand the progressive growth of awareness need never be impatient with their students, because a wise teacher realizes that telling a student of his errors is a limited form of communication, addressed only to his mind. It takes longer for full awareness to pervade all three centers, giving the emotional impulse, mental clarity, and physical ability to change.

Preparation is the subject of the next chapter, which reminds me of the Five P Principle: Proper preparation prevents poor performance. As Millman puts it, "Preparation is the foundation for success." He uses a number of metaphors and anecdotes to settle this point in the mind of the reader. You can't build a strong house without first constructing a foundation. You can't run until you practice walking. You can't read this article without first learning the alphabet and the meaning of printed words and how they work together.

Millman suggests step-by-step, systematic preparation, and he points out that the concept of "difficulty" has no absolute meaning but is relative to one's personal state. What might be difficult for some might be easy for others, but all must engage in preparation in order to achieve the goal. In this context, he discusses choosing a teacher. While he might be talking about athletic coaches, the discussion applies to martial arts instructors, as well.

The next chapter is on developing talent. Contrary to popular opinion that states that talent is inborn, Millman says that talent can be developed. This is intimately tied to proper preparation, and through proper preparation, the "developed" athlete might become superior to the "natural" athlete who does not properly prepare. The fable of the Tortoise and the Hare is an extreme example.

The main element to developing talent, Millman says, is letting go. This advice is essentially the same as the Taiji dictum to relax, sink, and release. Part-and-parcel of this is the ability to focus on the matter at hand without extraneous thought interfering with either the physical or mental flow. Thus, the true natural athlete obtains a meditative state while in the midst of movement, opening his mind and body to the natural flows of natural laws. In short, you are what you believe you are, and if you believe you are more, you will become more.

Conversely, if you believe you can't, then you can't. The one major blockage to this natural flow is the illusory, the self-destructive self-concept that hinder not just athletic ability but one's entire life. Other negative self-concepts are fear of failure and destructive self-criticism, both of which warp and over-blow natural and rational mental states, transforming what is helpful into something harmful.

But there are tools beyond self-awareness that one can utilize to self-correct. One-pointed attention is one—a concept that should be familiar to Taiji and Aikido practitioners. Another is hypermotivation. This can be induced through hypnosis, but it also can be a completely conscious action, such as manifesting Aikido's "unbendable arm." Millman gives a couple of simple activities to help one further develop concentration.

Emotional talent is the subject of the next chapter, and Millman opens with the idea that emotional energy is the fire that fuels motivation, and it is motivation that fuels life. In fact, he says, motivation *is* emotional talent, and athletics/martial arts place more than average demands on the individual. To the extent that one develops emotionally, the activity, whatever it might be, is enhance. But that requires facing emotions—demons and all—to eliminate the dross and enhance the beneficial aspects. Once one does, then the normal negative emotions of fear, sorrow, and anger no longer sway the mind as strongly, helping release tensions we might not even be aware of. So, in the next section, Millman discusses ways to break the circuit of tension and gives some exercises or other modes of behavior that can help rid the body of tension.

Breathing is the subject of the next chapter, and Millman links the inspiration of breath to the concept of inspired thinking/behavior. Much of this is effected by linking the mind and body and paying attention to one's breathing patterns, adjusting them as necessary to relax the body and sink one's energy to the tantien. As with the section just before, he presents an exercise to help accomplish that.

If mental clarity lights the path, and emotional energy furnishes the fuel, the body becomes the vehicle for action, and physical talent is the subject of the next chapter. Millman writes:

> Because mind and emotions are difficult to observe and can be resistant to change, the body is an ideal medium to work with in developing whole-body talent. The body is a plastic form, which can be reshaped by the intelligent application of energy. Its state reflects—and influences—the nature of the mind and emotions.

Martial artists who have practiced for some time understand what Millman is talking about. Through practice over time, skills develop, and those skills—and awareness of them—fundamentally alter the martial artist's inner being. The primary skill to be developed is correct posture. Without correct posture, nothing will work right—not athletics, not sports, not martial arts, not dance or any other physical activity. In fact, Millman touches on how a person's posture can reveal information about that person's inner workings. He gives a couple of simple exercises to help improve posture before discussing resistance to change, which seems to be a perpetual human state.

The following chapter delves into diet. He writes:

> Diet is nothing more than a matter of simple, ordinary natural habits of eating. It doesn't require exotic programs or foods. Persistent, natural patterns of diet are the key, not puritan perfectionism; patterns which reflect the body's essential needs rather than the mind's cravings.

Millman then discusses relaxation at length: What is relaxation, and how do you achieve it? One way that might help is the relaxation method he gives instructions for, which is very much like Psycho-Cybernetics, a relaxation and fulfillment technique developed by Maxwell Maltz and presented in his 1960 book, *Psycho-Cybernetics*, which remains in print.

A discussion of strength comes next, and in it, the author points out that strength should be appropriate, not simple greater in quantity. To prove his assertion, he points to female gymnasts whose skills often exceed those of their male counterparts precisely because they don't carry muscle bulk that can inhibit movement. Instead of simply using pure strength, Millman says, the athlete should use internal energy to bolster the physical movements, making them, not stronger, but more powerful. He gives a couple of exercises to help the reader accomplish the work of using mental impulse to energize the physical body. This is exactly how Taiji accomplishes power.

Another element is suppleness, but Millman says that stretching is only part of the answer to achieve suppleness. Just as important are release of tension and the proper mindset: If you 'ask' your body to grow more supple, it will—if you ask it nicely. To aid in growing more supple, he recommends that the reader take up an art that will assist in achieving that, such as Taiji, Aikido, or Yoga. However it is achieved, Millman says, suppleness is more important than strength.

Sensitivity is the subject of the next section. It begins with the old anecdote about the Taiji master who was so sensitive that a fly couldn't alight without him noticing and reacting. Actually, this idea is a restatement of the same principle of lightness and sensitivity espoused in one of the Taiji Classics. After extolling the virtues of sensitivity, Millman gives an exercise to help become aware of sensitivity and to increase it.

Stamina receives a similar treatment. He writes:

> Stamina is a perfect reflection of the law of accommodation—that a demand over a period of time creates a specific development.

Stamina, he writes, also is a natural response to training and is a function of relaxation, strength, and suppleness. In other words, it takes time to get in shape. He writes.

Lawrence Morehouse, a UCLA researcher, and other colleagues have found that in four weeks of inactivity, you can lose 80 percent of your conditioning—and in four more weeks of progressive training, you can also regain 80 percent of your top fitness after being totally out of shape. If you progress very, very slowly, it may take more than four weeks. If you push it, you might shorten that time, but you're going to hurt.

Avoiding injuries is the topic of the next chapter, and Millman says:

> Injury is *always* the result of a fundamental weakness in a mental, emotional, or physical area of talent (or a combination of these). "Accidents" aren't really accidents. If you injure yourself, or if someone else injures you, *someone* wasn't paying attention, was upset, or wasn't physically prepared. (In fact, these three variables account for all "accidents" in daily life which can be linked to human error.)

Thank goodness he qualified that statement, because I don't see how a one could be prepared for a landslide, say, which obviously is an accident not cause by "human error."

Next, Millman discusses whole-body talent based on three centers within the individual, the most important of which is one's grounding to Earth. He writes:

> Always keep in mind what the natural athlete knows: that physical ability alone, without development of mental clarity and emotional energy, is a hollow accomplishment.

The next chapter, "The Techniques of Training," doesn't really discuss training techniques but rather training methodologies. Millman writes:

> What I want to convey...are the fundamental, general techniques of learning any and every form of movement. No matter what activity you practice, you'll be able to apply the following approaches and strategies.

These approaches and strategies are:

1) Warm-up
2) Learning how to learn
3) Awareness and practice
4) The stages of practice
5) Ideomotor action and mental practice
6) Slow-motion practice
7) Part-whole practice
8) The programming principle
9) Imitation

Each of these is treated to extensive explanations that bring them into focus and show how they are applicable to daily life as well as to athletics and the martial arts.

Chapter eight discusses competition, in both its positive and negative aspects. The best way to look at competition, Millman writes, is to ignore the confrontational aspects in favor of considering the competition to be a learning experience. Taken this way, it doesn't matter if you "win" or "lose" since, in either case, you've learned or further developed skill. And in competition, proper preparation is vital, and much of that preparation has to be focus.

Chapter nine digresses on the nature of sport at the current time, but it also projects into the future to envision new types of sports or games. He says that two questions need to be asked by anyone approaching a sport in a natural and healthy way:

1) Does this sport effectively contribute to the physical and psychological well-being of the athlete?
2) Does this sport develop heightened capacity for daily life?

He says that we all can look at our own strengths and weaknesses under the same lens to assess the value of the sport(s) with which we engage. He then suggests symmetrical training to help the individual reach full potential in his or her chosen activity. Such equilateral training is particularly necessary for those engaged in sports or activities that primarily use one side of the body, such as tennis, bowling, and others. He suggests several "new" sports that would help alleviate this problem, one of which he calls Taiji-Do, which is intended to encourage evasion and blending rather than clashing with an opponent.

The penultimate chapter is "Psycho-Fitness," and it defines the "master" of any art as a person who is the product of thorough psycho-physical training. To illustrate his point, he tells a lengthy anecdote about a Japanese master of the Tea Ceremony who was challenged to a sword duel by a master swordsman. Knowing nothing of swordplay, the master of the Tea Ceremony went to the famed swordsman, Miyamoto Musashi for advice on how to die properly. Miyamoto informed him that, as he was already a master of something, he could just as easily be master of something else, including the sword. All he had to do was hold the sword and express his mastery. At the duel, the master of the Tea Ceremony followed Miyamoto's advice and, filling his frame with mastery, raised his sword. In the light glinting from its blade, the master swordsman saw his own death, and he lowered his own sword and bowed in defeat to the master of the Tea Ceremony.

The point of the story is that, once one gains mastery over one art or subject or activity, that sense of mastery becomes ingrained and can be expressed other endeavors. This leads to a lengthy discussion on the life lessons that can be gained from physical activities, such as athletics or martial arts, and how those seep into and influence every aspect of one's being.

The final chapter is on how the three centers—mental, emotional and physical—can work together to not only enhance performance, but to place one within the "zone"—that mindless state of pure action and reaction in which the athlete does not actively participate but simply observes the action even as his body performs as close to perfection possible. Millman likens that state to satori, which he says brings the athlete both pleasure and satisfaction.

The Warrior Athlete is replete with information, but more, it serves as the voice of an excellent and experienced coach who knows how to prepare and motivate his team and the individual players on it. And no wonder, considering the author's credentials. Athletes can benefit greatly from this book, but martial artist of all stripes—particularly Taiji and Aikido practitioners—can, too, since the concepts apply to all physical activities.

Notes
1 "Dan Millman." *Wikipedia*, https://en.wikipedia.org/wiki/Dan_Millman

PART II

Meditation

On Silent Meditation

By Wan Laisheng
(Originally from Chapter Six of Wan's *Collection of Martial Arts Traditions*, 1929. *Brennan Translations*, 2020, 34 pages)

Although the title implies that the topic of this manual is (seated) meditation, only the first seven pages are devoted to that subject. The remainder depicts what the author calls "Playful Daoist Exercises," which are a combination of light chi kung and self-massage.

Wan begins with a general introduction to seated meditation in which he names the benefits, which include better physical health, less tension, and nourishment of the spirit.

Next, he covers methods of seated meditation, starting with a few basic precepts such as posture, breathing, and attention. Three seated postures are demonstrated, then Wan takes the reader through the process of preparing for, approaching, and engaging in seated meditation. He speaks to a number of important points, including the positions of the hands, tongue, and eyes, and attention to the elixir field (tantien). Then he does the same for elements to attend to when emerging from the meditative state.

All this is pretty basic, and folks interested in meditation might find some of this helpful—or simply too elementary or sketchy compared to the depth of treatment featured in full-length books on the subject.

The light chi kung material appears next, and it includes a Taoist exercise for preventing eye disease, a chi kung called "A Thousand-Eight Hundred Accumulations" intended to rid the practitioner of illness, and yet another Taoist method for ridding illness and invigorating the body. Some of these exercises involve internal energy work, but others are basically just physical manipulations. For similar material covered much more thoroughly, see, *The Book of Internal Exercises*, by Stephen T. Chang with Richard C. Miller, reviewed earlier in this volume.

The Tao of Meditation
Way to Enlightenment

By Jou Tsung Hwa
(Tai Chi Foundation, 1983, 176 pages)

Despite Jou Tsung Hwa's scanty output, he is, in my opinion, a giant among Taiji authors, thanks to his *The Tao of Tai-Chi Chuan: Way to Rejuvenation*, one of the first really excellent books on the art in English. Apparently, I'm not the only one. He appeared at the masters demonstration for Jeff Bolt's United States National Chinese Martial Arts Competitions in 1989 and, upon his introduction, received a spontaneous standing ovation from the crowd of close to a thousand onlookers. Jou also founded the Tai Chi Farm, which, for several decades, hosted high-caliber Taiji retreats. *The Tao of Meditation* is book two of the author's The Tao Series, which consists of the aforementioned *The Tao of Tai-Chi Chuan* and the later *The Tao of I Ching: Way to Divination*.

The Tao of Meditation opens, appropriately enough, with several photos of figures in meditation: one of the author in a seated posture and three of giant Buddha statues in seated or standing postures. The gestalt of these photos helps make the words that follow less important than the results they might help inspire, which can be seen in the serenity of the figures' features.

The book is divided roughly into two halves, each consisting of two chapters. The first two chapters delve into philosophical territory as they lay out the background and precepts of understanding and working with internal energy. This information would be of interest to anyone practicing Taiji or, indeed, any of the other internal martial arts or even yoga. The book's second half is a discussion of methodological foundations and techniques. Though its information is necessarily basic in terms of techniques—those being best learned from a live teacher—it is long on the methodology, laying a firm foundation for future progress in meditation.

Jou opens with a short introduction that defines the Tao.... Okay, you can't really define the Tao, but he explains that we use the word to refer to the base substance and force of the universe before they separated into substance and force. From there, he quickly waxes philosophical in a most uplifting manner—eager to help the reader learn as much as possible to advance in any way he or she can. He writes:

> How can we discover those gifts which nature bestows on each one of us?.... We must look within ourselves, not once, but again, and again, and again, to discover those things about ourselves that are most important to us.

He continues in this humane tone to explain the background of meditation and many of the reasons to practice the art. Interestingly, he makes an effort to de-link meditation from specific religions, saying:

> By helping us think clearly and concentrate fully, Ching Tso [meditation] enables us to commune totally with our God, without distracting or artificial thoughts.

Next he discusses approaching meditation from a scientific standpoint. He writes:

> To use scientific knowledge to understand meditation, is, as the Chinese proverb says, 'To scratch an itching foot with the boot on.'

Science, in other words, can monitor heart rate, brain waves, and the like, but it can never pierce the veil to the infinitue on the "other side" of the meditator's mind. The problem for science is that the "other side" is not like it is here and is not amenable to measurement.

As proof, we have been afforded glimpses of more "tangible" places where the reality we know vanishes into we know not what. We call them black holes, and there's no telling what lies beyond their event horizons. Or what lies beyond the farthest distance that we can see with our telescopes in the visual and radio spectrums. And if the universe is constantly expanding, its farthest distance is, in itself, a vanishing horizon. More to the point, very few of us can truly see into our own souls. But Jou points out that we do have a way to actually do that, and it's called meditation.

Chapter one is "Yin-Yang and Tai-Chi." By Tai-Chi, he does not mean the martial and meditative art but rather the concept of duality acting in unison as one, as in the taijitu, the tai chi symbol. He begins by discussing the Chinese philosophy of yin and yang, and his explanations are thorough and illustrative. They are geared, however, more for those who do not yet have a grounding in these concepts, and more-knowledgeable readers might find themselves skimming, like a bird over water, looking for a good fish to dive down after. But that doesn't mean that Jou's discussions and explanations are facile, just basic, and he employs a large enough school of fish to keep even the more knowledgable reader diving in repeatedly. Ironically enough, some of his explanations are scientifically based, but such is the way of yin and yang within our state of reality.

Things get more interesting when Jou talks about how yin and yang interact to creatively form reality. This begins with the yin aspects of creativity, which are mental, and gradually transitioning them into the yang aspects, which are physical. The lessons of this section apply to Taiji in demonstrating how passive mental images can transition, through the intent-driven energy of chi, into physical force.

He continues extolling the virtues and applicability of yin/yang philosophy for several more pages, growing both more cosmic and more abstract and carrying the reader along with him. Then he comes back to Earth with the simple question, "Who am I?" To answer this question, which probably has been asked by nearly every human who has ever lived, he begins at the beginning by considering the creation of humankind and moving on from there.

All of this is very philosophical, interesting, and informative, though sometimes, Jou's arguments don't work out. For example, in a discussion of God, he cites the religious skeptic's argument:

> If God created the universe, where is God? If I do not know God, I cannot believe He created the universe.

Jou's response is:

> This is a meager argument because we could counter that question with another question: 'Do you know the creator of the fie hydrant? Of not, can you believe that it was in fact designed by someone?'

This is, to use Jou's own adjective, a meager counter. In the first place, we cannot physically touch or even see, much less encompass, God and the totality of reality. However, we can touch a fire hydrant and embrace it nearly fully within our arms. We cannot know where God or reality came from, but we can watch a crew install a fire hydrant and follow them back to the public works building where the fire hydrant came from and where others are stored. We can learn what companies manufacture hydrants, and with some diligent research, we most likely could discover just who did design the fire hydrant. Birdsill Holly Jr., died April 27, 1894, was an American mechanical engineer and inventor of water hydraulics devices. He is known for inventing mechanical devices that improved city water systems and patented an improved fire hydrant that is similar to those used currently for firefighting.[1]

But no matter how hard we look, no matter how deeply we delve into things or how far outward we look, we can't go back to the moment of creation and watch it unfold, nor can we see forward to the end of space-time. Without being able to do either of those, science can never make a definitive statement about the totality of reality. For them to do that, they would have to stand outside of reality, which would fundamentally alter the reality into something else. The eyes of Heisenberg, after all.

For the most part, however, Jou's arguments and statements are valid, and the tenor his discussion/explanation/speculation is highly philosophical, and for those of us who like to engage that sort of thing, it's mostly interesting. I say "mostly" because a lot of what he's talking about is, again, aimed at the less experienced and knowledgable reader, so I sometimes found myself skimming explanations of something I already know about. But not always, because Jou has a knack for telling anecdotes and employing a witty sense of humor that has an occasional nip, all of which make for entertaining reading even if you already know the story.

Next, Jou delves into the dimensions—the three spatial and time—to lay the groundwork for the concept of extra-dimensionality. His discussions of the three spatial dimensions—length, width, and depth—begin with the French philosopher and mathematician, René Descartes, who provided a mathematical way to define the three spatial dimensions by representing them as three graduated axes—X, Y, and Z. As with the previous chapter, the text is aimed at those with little background in these matters, which also were thoroughly covered in Edwin A. Abbott's novel, *Flatland*, first published in 1884. Abbott's primary purpose was to satirize Victorian society, but the book's more lasting contribution was its clear description of what perception might be like for sentient beings living in one or two-dimensional worlds. What would it be like for those beings to encounter objects or beings from more complex dimensions, such as our three-dimensional reality?

Jou's examples aren't exactly those employed by Abbott, but they are necessarily very similar, so if you have a clear sense of Abbott's argument, you can skip much of this section, which ends in another skippable passage that is a retelling of the famous parable of the "Blind Men and the Elephant." I say you can skip this material if you know it already, but that doesn't at all mean it isn't cogent or germane to Jou's intent. Immediately after, Jou winds up the chapter with an interesting discussion on the *Flatland* parable from a theoretical four-dimensional point of view. What would our three-dimensional reality seem like to a being who exists within four-dimensional space?

That fourth dimension, time, is the subject of the next section. What is it? That depends, Jou says, on how you look at time, and he proceeds to discuss several ways that time can be viewed and experienced. And since we three-dimensional beings can, to some extent, manipulate length, width, and height, Jou wonders what time would seem like to a four-dimensional being for whom time is a common and manipulable element of its environment?

Jou also wonders if time is always constant in its display/flow within the real world. Science has definitively proved that it is not, but Jou demonstrates the same fact by inference. To illustrate his points, Jou uses simple examples, and he also relates a couple of Chinese stories on time. In the first, a man dreams an entire and vivid lifetime during a few minutes of sleep, and in the second, a man becomes so engrossed in an external activity that he looses all sense of time and stagnates as the world changes around him—a sort of Rip Van Winkle story. Jou concludes this section by noting that we humans are stuck in our three-dimensional world and remain subject to the fourth dimension of time. This, he finishes, "is the space in which we live."

Since Jou has consistently addressed the Really Big Questions, it's no wonder that he continues with a chapter titled, "Where Can We Find the Truth?" He opens with Chuang Tzu's famous passage in which the sage tells of dreaming that he was a butterfly and, upon awakening, was not sure if he was Chuang Tzu dreaming he was a butterfly or a butterfly dreaming he was Chuang Tzu. Truth is, after all, as relative as is time.

From there, Jou moves on to a discussion that takes in yin and yang as a constant state of change, transformation, and alternation, all within the constraints of time. This is a fairly deep discussion that includes clear examples of the cyclic nature of the universe.

As if all this wasn't philosophical enough, the the first chapter of the second half of the book is actually titled, "Philosophy." Perhaps all the foregoing should have been subsumed in a section titled, "Background and Philosophy of Meditation," and the present chapter titled, "The Process, Methodology, and Technology of Meditation," for those are what these chapters cover, beginning with "The Goal of Meditation." The subsequent discussion includes a number of practical reasons to practice meditation, from its promotion of physical health all the way to its providing a path for spiritual enlightenment. Included are clues about impediments to clearing one's body and mind not just of tension, but of physical, emotional, and psychic blockages that impeded the flow of chi within the self.

A discussion of Zen and one of the tools it uses to achieve enlightenment—the Koan—comes next. After definitions and descriptions of the precepts of Zen, Jou relates several famous Koans, all of which are germane to Jou's arguments. In the last subsection in this chapter, "The First Stage of Enlightenment," Jou does not go into the specific methodology or technology of meditation, but rather its process—how one develops through meditation over time. As with other chapters and subsections, this one has its share of stories, most notably here about the Buddha and his development from a worldly child of wealth and power into the exact opposite: an enlightened being. Again, the stories and anecdotes help illustrate the pedagogical points Jou is making, particularly the stories about his own life as a malnourished child and refugee from Communist China. His personal experiences and subsequent development are both illustrative and inspirational.

The second chapter of the second half of the book is titled simply, "Meditation." Its purpose is to supply the methodology and technology of meditation. This book, however, isn't exactly a how-to manual, but rather a "this is the way it's done when you're starting out, and what you can expect as you progress" sort of book. It defines the meditation environment, which includes not just what's around the meditator, but what the meditator is seated on. Next come a handful of drawing showing specific seated or lying postures, followed by a set of twelve seated chi kung exercises that are mostly stretching, though a few are simply postural.

The following subchapter covers the Microcosmic Orbit, which is the body's main chi circuit. For those who don't know, Jou tells us that it consists of two channels called vessels. The Conception Vessel runs from the tip of the tongue, down the front of the front of the body through the digestive tract, to the perineum, and the Governing Vessel runs from the tip of the tailbone, up the spine and through the top of the brain, then down to the hard palate. The goal of meditation is to empower the flow of chi energy through the Microcosmic Orbit, increasing it in both quantity and strength until it breaks through the psychic barriers at the top of the head and fountains forth to merge with cosmic consciousness, producing enlightenment. This is a major difference in the treatment of chi by meditators and by Taijiquanists. The purpose of Taiji practice is to strengthen the chi but also to maintain its circular flow through the Microcosmic Orbit and, further, to willfully empower the chi through the network of channels, or circuits, in the limbs referred to as the Macrocosmic Orbit.

This is a pretty intense discussion of value to Taijiquanists, other internal martial artists, and yoga enthusiasts as well as to meditators, though, obviously, it's geared for the latter. The subchapter includes snippets from a novice meditator's diary, indicating his rapid advancement over the course of just a few months—included, I suppose, partially as a roadmap for the reader, but also as an endorsement of the method of meditation in producing tangible effects on those who take up the practice.

The next section discusses transferring chi and shen (spirit), and includes specific exercises to achieve further stages of development. The section after that discusses proceeding from shen to void and enlightenment. With that, Jou closes the book. After all, where can you go after enlightenment?

I can't really call *The Tao of Meditation* a manual on meditation, although it serves admirably for that purpose. Rather, it is a meditation on meditation. But it does contain enough practical information, methods, and exercises to get a novice meditator going, and all the intense philosophical material serves to prepare the meditator physically, intellectually, emotionally, and spiritually. The book also concludes with sage advice for anyone undertaking not just meditation, but any activity that builds or increases abilities: Learn valid techniques—which requires a good teacher, diligence, and persistence—but in the end, you are your own best teacher.

The author also recognizes that increasing or improving abilities, as with life itself, is not a matter of simple arithmetic progression but can become geometric—and often even allows the practitioner to take a quantum leap into a cosmic paradigm. That's what meditation is all about.

The Tao of Meditation, as with *The Tao of Tai-Chi Chuan*, is an excellent and thoughtful book that would be of value to any reader interested in pursuing any of the internal energy arts.

Notes

1. "Birdsill Holley." *Wikipedia*, https://en.wikipedia.org/wiki/Birdsill_Holly

Meditation
An Eight-Point Program

By Eknath Easwaran
(Nilgiri Press, 1978, 238 pages)

Meditation, by Eknath Easwaran, has two subtitles: the one shown above, which is on the book's front cover, and *Commonsense Directions for an Uncommon Life*, which appears on the title page. Both are accurate.

Eknath was born in 1910 into an ancient matrilineal Hindu family in a village in South India.[1] He was raised by his mother and grandmother, whom he regarded as his spiritual teacher. As a young man, he met and was influenced by Mahatma Gandhi, and he took up meditation, eventually developing his own form, know as Passage Meditation, which is meditating on passages taken from various religious and spiritual texts.

At age sixteen, following schooling in his village, he attended a small Catholic college near his home and then graduated from the larger University of Nagpur with degrees in English and law. He served as a professor at the University of Nagpur until 1959, when he came to the University of California, Berkeley, on a Fulbright Scholarship. There he taught what is thought to be the first credit course in meditation offered at a major university.

During the succeeding years, he married, founded the Ramagiri Ashram in Marin County, the Blue Mountain Center of Meditation, and Nigiri Press, which has published his more than thirty books.

His translations of the *Bhagavad Gita*, the *Upanishads*, and the *Dhammapada* are critically acclaimed, and his other books run the gamut from commentaries on the *Upanishads* to spiritual biographies and, of course, meditation.

As the subtitle on the front cover indicates, Eknath has distilled his meditation program to eight important points.

1) Meditation: Silent repetition upon memorized inspirational passages from one of the world's great religions. Practiced for one-half hour each morning.
2) The Mantram: Silent repetition of a mantram, holy name, or hallowed phrase from one of the world's great religions.
3) Slowing Down: Set priorities to reduce stress and hurry.
4) One-Pointed Attention: Give full concentration to whatever matter is currently at hand.
5) Training the Senses: Enjoy simple pleasures in order to avoid craving for unhealthy excess.
6) Putting Others First: Denounce selfishness and cultivate altruism.
7) Spiritual Companionship: Practice meditation in the company of others.
8) Reading the Mystics: Draw inspiration from the writings of the scriptures of all religions.

Early in the book, Eknath makes a basic statement about the relationship of meditation to reality:

> When people ask me if I can bend a key with my psychic energy, I simply confess, "I can't even bend one with my physical energy." When they ask me, "Did you come to this country in your astral body?" I say, "Air India actually… pleasant flight." If I want to find out what is on the other side of a steel door, I don't try to "see" through it; I open it. If I am chilly, I don't vibrate my limbs and call up astral powers; I put on a pullover.

From there, he defines what meditation is, first by saying what it is not: making your mind blank, hypnosis, or discursive thinking. It is, he says:

> A systematic technique for taking hold of and concentrating to the utmost degree our latent mental power. It consists of training the mind, especially attention and the will, so that we can set forth from the surface level of consciousness and journey into the very depths.

He then goes into the three stages of meditation and the realizations that flow from each: that we are not the body and we are not the mind. Only after those realizations, Eknath says, can we realize our deeper, truer self—a self that is part and parcel of the Universe. (Call it God or the Tao, if you wish.)

The next chapter covers how to begin meditation, including pacing, dealing with distractions, choosing spiritual passages to meditate on, time and place, holding postures, dealing with drowsiness, and understanding physical sensations that manifest during meditation. He also warns against the dangers that might arise, such as powerful emotions.

After that, he deals with the mantram, or mantra.

> A mantram is a spiritual formula of enormous power that has been transmitted from age to age in a religious tradition. The users, wishing to draw upon this power that calms and heals, silently repeat the words as often as possible during the day, each repetition adding to their physical and spiritual well-being.

In this chapter, Eknath discusses what a mantram can do and its function in meditation. He presents several great mantrams, then discusses how to choose and repeat them before going into how to deal with emotions that arise during meditation. Part of this is dealing with the powerful conditions of depression and crisis.

Slowing down is the subject of the next chapter, and here Eknath gives a lot of soothing talk about slowing down in one's life to help rid oneself of tensions and other dross that only serve to drag the individual down. Subchapters are titled: "Slowness and Sensitivity," "Hurry Sickness," and "The Competitive Drive," followed by subsections that give clues and ideas about how to deal with these issues.

Next we come to a matter of importance not just to meditators, but to all martial artists who practice internal styles and to some who practice external forms: One-Point Attention. This is awareness of and concentration of the attention on the tantien, which is the generator and repository of chi. This, he says, is as much a matter of training the mind as of training the body. He covers some of the benefits of One-Point Attention, the principal one being that in striving for One-Point Attention, one increases the power and focus of one's attention. He writes:

> Developing a one-pointed mind as suggested here will enrich your life moment by moment. You will find that your senses are keener, your emotions more stable, your intellect more lucid, your sensitivity to the needs of others heightened. Whatever you do, you will be there more fully.

Eknath then covers training the senses, which means training the mind to control the senses and not letting the senses do the controlling. For example, he goes into what he calls "Automatic Eating," which is the proclivity to eat even when one is not hungry. Aside from leading to possible negative physical consequences—obesity, high cholesterol, and diabetes, for example—it also demonstrates a lack of will, which can be strengthened through meditation.

Vigilance is another topic related to the will, which leads to the concept of choice with regards to behavior. But to chose sensibly, one must also deal with the power of conditioning, which can work against anyone trying to exert their will power in an alternate direction. This leads into the power of thoughts to either reinforce negative behaviors or to activate change.

Putting others first is the subject of the next chapter, and here Eknath delves into the ego, personality, love, patience, and mending estrangements. Spiritual companionship comes next, with Eknath talking about community cohesion and well-being. "Reading the Mystics," is the title of the last chapter, and in it, the author delves into the nature of mystical literature and gives a number of examples that the reader might find useful. More examples are in the appendix which follows immediately after.

Meditation is very well—and spiritually—written, with the author bringing in many quotes and ideas, not just from Hindu and Buddhist literature, but from authors and thinkers worldwide. Eknath was an important figure in introducing mediation to the West, and this book is a worthy document of his reasoning, precepts, and methodology. Recommended.

Notes

1 Biographical information comes from the mini bio in the book and from "Eknath Easwaran," *Wikipedia*, https://en.wikipedia.org/wiki/Eknath_Easwaran

PART III

Yoga

Yoga Made Easy
A Personal Yoga Program that Will Transform Your Daily Life

By Howard Kent
(Quarto Publishing Co., 1994, 160 pages)

This review should be simple to write since I have never practiced yoga and know very little about it beyond the basics known to most folks. My impression of the art is that it is most closely akin to the chi kung arts, which I do know a little about--mostly to Wai Dan, or external, chi kung, with many Nei Dan, or internal chi kung, elements mixed in. Notable among those is diaphragmatic breathing, which enhances and builds the internal energy of chi. Or perhaps I should call it "prana" when talking about yoga.

As with martial arts literature, there are many, many thousands of instructional volumes on yoga, not to mention additional thousands of videos on *Youtube* or DVD. Not being a yoga practitioner, I don't have many examples in my library, but I've owned *Yoga Made Easy* for many years, though I have not read until now. I don't know if it is any better or worse than other yoga manuals, but looking it over, I can see that it is interesting and well produced, and it covers a lot of ground that jibes with chi kung practices.

The book, which deals with Hatha Yoga, opens with an introduction that lays out the ideas behind yoga and yoga's principles and precepts. These include linking body and mind, achieving balance, and learning control of the body, breath, and mind. It also addresses the issue of whether or not yoga is a religion, arguing that it is not but giving the issue some play.

How to use the book and developing a personal program of yoga occupy the next couple of chapters. Since this book is intended for at-home instruction for those lacking an experienced instructor, a list of cautions and prohibitions is included.

The book, itself, is the program. Each of the subsequent twelve chapter covers one month of instruction, with exercises accumulating over the course of the year—hopefully with the abilities of the student increasing at the same pace. Remember folks, you gotta practice if you want to see results.

Beginning with simple stretching and toning exercises during month one, the book takes the novice through a course that becomes more rigorous but never impossibly so. All the exercises and concepts are well explained and accompanied by excellent color photos and drawings, and all the movements look easy to learn, even if they might not be easy to perform with facility in the beginning. But if one is patient and faithfully follows the course laid out by this book for the entire year, he or she should end up in really good shape.

I'm not going to go into each chapter/month of instruction except to say that each contains relevant information about the body, prana, and other aspects as well as instructions for the physical exercises. This allows the user to accumulate and integrate knowledge gradually along with technique and skill. Yoga, the author points out, is as much mental as it is physical, and the discipline is not simply about "exercise."

Yoga Made Easy would be an excellent introduction for anyone who doesn't, for one reason or another, have access to a live teacher. In many respects, yoga, like chi kung but unlike Taiji, can be learned on one's own because it is postural-based rather than movement-based—it is a routine. Not a form. The book is well written and well designed, but as I said earlier, I don't have an adequate number of yoga books to accurately gauge the quality of this one against others. But it you want to learn the basics of yoga, I have to say that this book will deliver the goods.

Weight Control through Yoga

By Richard L. Hittleman
(Bantam Books, 1971, 208 pages)

As with books on the martial arts, books on yoga can have origins anywhere from the expert to the questionable. *Weight Control through Yoga* is one of the former, and author Richard Hittleman has an impressive background.

Hittleman was born in 1927, took an MA in Oriental mysticism at Columbia University, and was friend with Paul Brunton and Alan Watts. By his early twenties, he'd become a pupil of the Indian spiritual master, Ramana Maharshi and also developed a strong interest in Buddhism and Zen. He believed that yoga and meditation were the path to enlightenment, and that the divine is present in all people.

> Self is another word for "God." This is the God who is the Absolute, immutable, without qualities, pure Awareness, without beginning or end.[1]

In the 1960s and 1970s, Hittleman's books, lectures, recordings, and TV programs brought yoga to more people than anyone else alive at the time. Millions viewed his program, *Yoga for Health*, and read his nearly twenty books. Specializing in Hatha Yoga, he also taught Bhakti, Raja, and Karma Yoga. Apparently he had a talent for taking beginners and successfully leading them into more advanced physical asanas as well as imparting the profound philosophy of Advaita Vedanta.[1]

Hittleman's expertise and exposure brought him into contact with many people with physical issues, quite often weight. He writes in the introduction:

> I have had the opportunity not only to suggest various applications of the Yoga techniques to the problem of obesity, but to learn directly from these viewers the results they attained.... Here, for the first time in written form, we offer the plan that has been tested the most extensively and found to be the most successful.

Hittleman opens with a chapter on how his yoga weight-loss plan differs from others. It must, he says, include a sensible diet as well as physical exercise, but he says that yoga also offers a philosophy that is different from the average strategy of dieting and fasting. What makes his plan work, he says, is that it is a combination of exercise, nutrition, and encouragement.

He starts his "patient" off with fasting in order, he says, to lose up to 10 percent of total weight during the first week. Having fasted a little, myself, I can attest to the efficacy of this method to immediately lose some weight and to help reduce the body's reliance on larger intakes of food. The main pitfall is in relapsing through gorging. Once the body is used to a lesser intake, eating less will become more natural.

Hittleman presents several fasting plans: the Partial Fast, the Liquid Fast, and the Total Fast. The first two have menus of acceptable foods and amounts, but of course, the last does not. A question-and-answer session on the three fasting plans comes next, and that is followed by helpful hints to observe while fasting.

The next section of the book covers three exercise routines, each more advanced than the previous one. Full explanations of the reasoning behind the exercises are included. The models for the photos might not be seriously obese, but they certainly aren't svelte, yet you see them in fairly difficult poses. That's an element of the "encouragement" part. Charts for personalizing these routines winds up the chapter.

The instructions for the routines, which take up the lion's share of the book, come next, and the exercises are thoroughly described in text and excellent line drawings. Breathing methodology also is discussed.

The final, long chapter is on nutrition. It first discusses the yoga food regimen, then the author presents notes about various foodstuff, from fruits and vegetables to dairy products, meat and poultry, beverages, nuts, and many more. The book ends with a two-week menu.

I've never had much of a problem with my weight, but if I did, this looks like a good program to take up. The exercises are progressive, beginning with the simple and moving to the more strenuous to help the would-be yogi transition from weakness to strength —mentally as well as physically. The book's cover calls them "life changing." Maybe. That's up to you.

As of this writing, this book is out of print, but used copies can be found online.

Notes
1. "Richard Hittleman." *Wikipedia*, https://en.wikipedia.org/wiki/Richard_Hittleman

PART IV

Archery

Archery Principles

By Qi Jiguang (and Yu Dayou)
(Originally Chapter 13 of *New Book of Effective Methods*, 1560. Brennan Translations, 2021, 8 pages)

The brevity of this manual can be explained by its original status as a single chapter of an entire book on the martial arts: *New Book of Effective Methods* (aka, *New Book on Effective Military Techniques*), by the famous 16th-century general and martial artist,Qi Jiguang. Although there already were references to the martial arts in various writings during Qi's time, the original edition of his book, printed by woodblock, is considered to be the oldest extant martial arts manual.[1] (See the review of General Qi's, *The Boxing Classic: Keys to Nimbleness*, for the earliest depiction of an open-hand form in Volume III of this series.)

Archery Principles delivers as advertised, being a collection of precepts, methodologies, and ideas on the mindset necessary for archery. Included are methods of holding the bow, drawing it, and releasing the arrow. Errors are pointed out and encouragement is delivered. The author also spends some time on maintaining one's equipment, which includes:

> Keep your horse well-fed, well-trained, and obedient. Teach it not to be startled by any object in its path and not to turn sharply while galloping.

Crude antique drawings illustrate two methods of drawing the bow, and these end the book.

Will this book help teach you archery? Probably not, but beginning archers and historians of archery might be interested in what it has to say.

Notes

1 *Chinese Martial Arts Training Manuals: A Historical Survey.* Brian Kennedy and Elizabeth Guo (Blue Snake Books, 2005), p. 94.

Archery

By Wayne C. McKinney
(William C. Brown Co. Publishers, 1966, 106 pages)

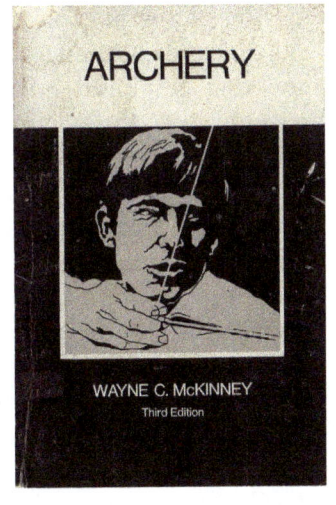

Back in the day, I did a bit of archery, and I bought a couple of books to give me some pointers. Wayne C. McKinney's, *Archery*, was one. The author was head of the Health and Physical Education Department at Southwest Missouri State University, a prolific author of fitness-related books, and a member of the Research Council of the American Alliance of Health, Physical Education, and Recreation.

This is the kind of book you read for solid information, and this one delivers, opening with a chapter on archery tackle that thoroughly describes every element of archery equipment that existed at the time. It's important to note that sport archery has evolved significantly since the writing of this book—so much so that contemporary bows and release mechanisms seem completely alien to a person used to seeing the bow as a simple, though dynamic, weapon.

The author describes arrows in their variety of shafts, fletching, and points. The bow is described next—or rather, bows, since there is variety here, too. He goes into the materials, construction, size, draw weight, and strings, and includes accessories like stabilizers, sights, arm guards, and quivers. Care of archery tackle finishes the chapter.

Fundamentals of target archery is the subject of the second chapter. It begins with "bracing," or, stringing the bow, and it gives several methods the archer can use to accomplish that. Nocking the arrow, holding the bow with the arrow nocked, and drawing the bow come next, and the explanations include choosing an anchor point—the place on the archer's face where the hand touches when the bow is fully drawn. Aiming methods are featured next, including advice on correcting bow sights and aim, and this is followed by releasing the bow and follow-through. Scoring finishes out the chapter.

The next chapter is on archery as a sport, which begins by describing different types of matches, each with specific numbers of arrows fired at specific distances. Then come descriptions of field archery, flight shooting, and Olympic archery.

Chapter four is on bow hunting and fishing. First up is a discussion of the differences between the tackle used for sport archery and that employed in bow hunting. Types of hunting arrows are covered next, then techniques. The author highly recommends that bow hunters start practicing well before the hunting season opens in order to condition themselves for strength and accuracy.

Chapter five covers the evolution of archery from the Paleolithic Period to modern times. This is a fairly thorough account that illustrates the development of not just archery and its equipment, but its growing use on the battlefield prior to the introduction of firearms. Battles are recounted, famous archers have their moment, and finally the gun has its day. But the author points out that the bow is still an effective weapon where stealth is important.

Archery in literature and art is the subject of the next chapter. The literary references begin with the Greeks naming the constellation Sagittarius, which they imagined as a centaur shooting a bow. And there is another constellation named, simply, Saggita, or, the Arrow, which was supposed to be the arrow that Apollo used to kill the Cyclops. Apollo wasn't the only Greek god to be associated with the bow. Heracles (Hercules) bore an unusually powerful bow that he used often in the myths about him, including killing Paris with an arrow. During that same war, Achilles was killed by a poisoned arrow. And let's not forget Cupid, whose bow delivers love instead of death.

The literary references continue with Robin Hood, William Tell, James Fenimore Cooper's Leatherstocking Tales, Longfellow's famous poem, "Hiawatha," and many more. The references to the bow and arrow continue in art, which probably has far more examples than literature. From the Bayeux Tapestries to modern times, archery has been a staple feature of depictions of war and sport. The importance of many of these images, the authors contend, is that they reveal concepts of archery form and depictions of historic archery tackle.

The potential benefits of archery occupy the final chapter, and as with most martial arts, there is a degree of muscular development, hand-eye coordination, and one-point attention. Actually, there is one more chapter after this one, but it more properly should be termed a glossary, for it contains the the terminology of archery. Amusingly since the author is an educator, the book ends with a test on archery fundamentals, so he must have intended this to be a textbook.

There must be hundreds of how-to archery books out there, though I haven't seen many of them. This one helped me out when I was fiddling around with archery, and it might help you, too. It's well written, informative, and sufficiently illustrated to give the beginner some substance to his or her practice.

Encyclopedia of Archery

By W. F. Paterson
(St. Martin's Press, 1984, 216 pages)]

There's not much to be said about W. F. Paterson, *Encyclopedia of Archery*, since the title says it all.

Considering all the advancements modern archery has made since the writing of this book, a newer edition might contain them if there was one, but there isn't. Author W. F. Paterson was long-serving chairman of the Society of Archer-Antiquaries in England, and his previous book was *Saracen Archery* (with J. D. Latham).

As advertised, this is an encyclopedia that covers archery terms, but those occupy only the first half of the book. The second half is taken up with appendices, the first and longest on the constitution and rules of the International Archery Federation, now known as the World Archery Federation. After those come the shorter rules for the National Archery Association of the United States. I'm sure that, along with advancements in archery since this book was written, there have been at least a few rule changes in both organizations.

The next appendix is on champions up to the date of the book. While this list of archers is undoubtedly of historical interest, it is, by now, completely obsolete. The last three appendices are on equipment suppliers and archery organizations, and this material also is obsolete. There is no index.

This would be a fine source for definitions of archery and archery tackle, and used copies are still available online, but I'm sure that more-contemporary encyclopedic works on archery are available.

PART V

Research Resources

Acupuncture Medicine
Its Historical and Clinical Background

by Yoshiaki Omura, ScD, MD
(Japan Publications, Inc., 1982, 288 pages)

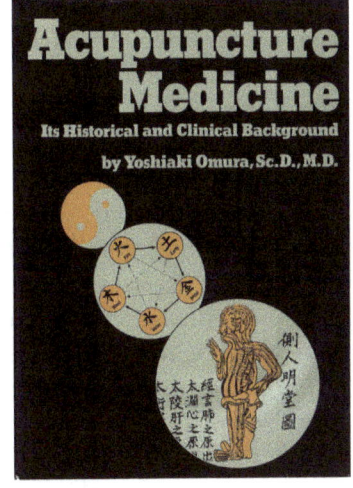

Any serious student of the internal martial arts—maybe any martial art—needs a good reference book on the meridian system. I realized this early in my Taiji practice, and just out at that time was *Acupuncture Medicine* by Yoshiaki Omura. This large-format hardback is essentially a textbook on the meridian system, and the information is relatively technical, but it is a useful reference for the layman, as well.

The book opens with a historical background on acupuncture and Chinese medicine. This includes a fairly detailed account of the foundational texts of traditional Chinese medicine, the oldest of which is purported to have been written by China's Yellow Emperor, Huang Ti, as long ago as four thousand years. Next, the author reviews several historical concepts of Oriental medicine from a linguistic standpoint, such as "medicine," "acupuncture," "moxibustion," "disease," and "chi." This material would be most relevant to those with an interest in the Chinese language and the development of these concepts.

Chapter two covers the anatomical and pathophysiological concepts of Oriental medicine. The discussion begins with a description of the six "solid/yang" organs and the six "hollow/yin" organs, which make up the basis for the twelve meridians of the Macrocosmic Orbit. Each one is described and linked with corresponding organs as defined by Western medicine. A number of historical illustrations accompany the descriptions to help give a sense of how an understanding of the meridian system developed over time.

This leads into a discussion of the meridian system itself and the acupuncture points through which the system can be affected and the chi flow manipulated. An extensive chart details how acupuncture points have been understood over time, giving their names in Chinese, Japanese, and English and their locations on particular meridians. Another chart shows the sequence of chi movement from one meridian to another during the course of the day, including times when it is most powerfully present in a given meridian/organ. Another extensive chart summarizes the pathways of the twelve main meridians and the diseases of the associated organs that can be treated.

Following that are twelve subchapters that discuss each of the twelve meridians in great detail, showing the pathways of each meridian, the organs affected by that meridian, and all the acupuncture points along the meridian. Included is a description of the illnesses or diseases that can be treated by stimulating given points. Each meridian is illustrated by two drawings: one old, historical version and one modern rendering.

The Microcosmic Orbit—the circuit composed of the Conception Vessel and the Governing Vessel—is similarly described before the author moves on to detail eight extra meridians and their key acupuncture points. Diseases of these ancillary meridians appear in a three-page list.

Chapter three deals with the classical pathophysiological concepts of Oriental medicine. It begins with the method with which classical Oriental medicine classifies disease, which is divided into three factors: external factors, internal factors, and those factors that cannot be defined as either external or internal. The six external factors, sometimes referred to as "evil chi," are: wind, cold, heat, moisture, dryness, and fire. The five internal factors are considered to be excessive expressions of five emotions, and each is linked to a particular organ, to a particular element from the Chinese theory of five elements, and to a particular color. They are:

Anger/liver/green or dark blue/wood
Joy/heart/red/fire
Worry/spleen/yellow/earth
Sadness/lung/white/metal
Fear/kidney/black/water

Following this is a discussion of clinical diagnosis of "fullness" and "emptiness" from the patient's symptoms and a detailed section on the five-element theory and its application in classical Oriental medicine.

Diagnostic methods in Oriental medicine are the subject of chapter four, which occupies more than one hundred pages. The individual topics include diagnosis by visual inspection of the eyes and skin, examination of the tongue, and analysis of the hands and feet, including fingers/toes, nails, palm/sole, and joints. Readers with a background in Reflexology will find much of interest here. Diagnosis by hearing comes next, and this is followed by a section on the importance of questioning the patient and assessing the patient's emotional and mental states. A six-page chart lays out many of the more important symptoms that can be determined by questioning the patient.

Analyzing the pulse is described next, and the text provides extensive information on an incredible great number of pulse points and how the physician can determine a patient's condition through them and their internal relationships. This is followed by methods to diagnose by palpitation and abdominal examination. Diagnosis by examination of the ear and its "topography" winds up the chapter, and the book's conclusion comes next.

Acupuncture Medicine isn't the sort of book you just read. It's best thought of as a text for intensive study or as a reference work. Much of the material is probably too detailed for the layman, but much of it is useful to anyone interested in the meridian system. You won't learn how to become a traditional Chinese physician from this book, but it's easy to see that practitioners of traditional Chinese medicine might use this book or one similar to it as part of their training. Over the years, I have gone back to it time and again as I've striven to understand, from a practical standpoint, the meridian system and its operation, and it has served me well.

The Body Electric
Electromagnetism and the Foundation of Life

by Robert O. Becker, M.D., and Gary Selden
(Quill, 1985, 366 pages)

There are only a few non-movement art books among these reviews, but occasionally, a book is just too significant to Taijiquanists—and others—to pass up, even if it isn't directly related to movement. *The Body Electric: Electromagnetism and the Foundation of Life,* by Dr. Robert O. Becker and Gary Selden, is one of them. It, along with *The Second Brain,* by Dr. Michael D. Gershon (reviewed next) were critical in helping me formulate what I consider to be a pretty sound theory of how chi is generated in the tantien and propelled through the meridian system. (I lay out this theory in *The Wellspring: An Inquiry into the Nature of Chi.*)

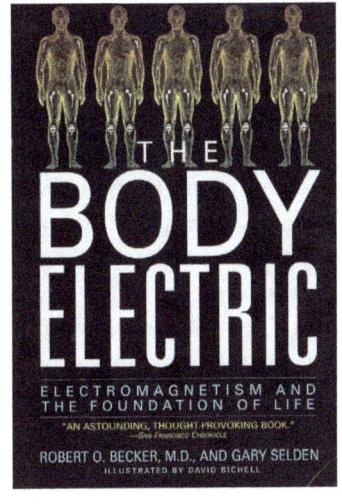

Becker is a research physician who was initially interested in the ability to regenerate lost limbs exhibited by salamanders, newts, and starfish, among others. He thought that if he could identify the mechanism of regeneration, it might be applied to higher forms of life, such as humans. He didn't manage to do that—though who knows what the future might hold—but he did something that might be more important. His book gives a scientific rationale for the structure and functioning of the Governing Vessel, which along with the Conception Vessel, forms the principal chi circuit in the body called the Microcosmic Orbit. (The rationale for the Conception Vessel comes from Gershon's book.)

Like Gershon's book, *The Body Electric* isn't a scientific text but a journey of scientific discovery for the general reader. It encompasses almost the entire history of scientific research into the phenomenon of bioelectricity, from the first detection of the effects of electricity on creature bodies, to the understanding that our bodies produce microcurrents, to the realization that these electrical pulses are part-and-parcel of our physical being. Wow, is this interesting stuff! And engrossingly told by Becker and Selden in this well-illustrated volume.

Becker didn't start out to discover anything about chi. In fact, when he began, he knew nothing about it. But interestingly, when he first learned about the concept of chi and the meridian system, he did not, as many scientists might, thrust the idea away like an unpalatable meal. Instead, he looked into it and discovered that a great number of specific acupuncture points could be mapped electrically. In fact, among the other vital stuff in this book, he was prescient enough to include a discussion of the potentially negative effects of microwave radiation from walkie-talkies and CB radios on the human body, presaging by twenty years the similar debate about risks posed by cell phones.

This is not just a good and extremely interesting book. It's an important one and a must-read for the serious Taiji enthusiast.

The Second Brain
A Groundbreaking New Understanding of Nervous Disorders of the Stomach and Intestines

by Michael D. Gershon, M.D.
(Quill, 1998, 320 pages)

It's rare that I'll review a book in this series that isn't about a martial or movement art, but Dr. Michael D. Gershon's *The Second Brain* is just too important to ignore. It does not mention chi or Taiji, or any other martial or movement art, but the basic content of the book is highly relevant to all of them.

Gershon was a research physician who specialized in the intestines, and he earned a place in medical history by identifying serotonin as a neurotransmitter and discovered that the vast majority of serotonin is produced in the intestines—in fact, in the exact location of the tantien.

I discovered the book through a happy fluke. I'd been struggling to understand the mechanism of the Microcosmic Orbit—the principal circuit of chi flow within the body. It is composed of the body's two major meridians: the Governing Vessel, which runs from the perineum, up the spine, and through the top of the head to the roof of the mouth, and the Conception Vessel, which starts at the tip of the tongue and runs down through the front of the body, through the tantien, to the perineum.

I felt I had a fairly decent grasp of the idea that chi is related to the body's bioelectrical output thanks to Dr. Robert O. Becker's T*he*

Body Electric: Electromagnetism and the Foundation of Life (reviewed above). Becker was a research physician who was interested in the mechanism of limb regeneration exhibited by newts, salamanders, and starfish, among others. Could it be possible, he wondered, to stimulate regeneration of limbs in higher forms of life, such as humans? His research into this led him to discover a great deal that was not yet known about the importance of bioelectricity naturally generated by the body

I go more into Becker's book in my review of it and in my book, *The Wellspring: An Inquiry into the Nature of Chi*, but the brunt of his research pointed to the idea that chi is, if not bioelectricity, then closely related to it. Being a researcher into nerves, Becker concentrated on the spine and brain. These are, of course, analogous to the Governing Vessel, so I figured I had a pretty good handle on that as a principal conduit for chi. But the Conception Vessel was an entirely different matter. No spine or brain in that location. Nothing but a bunch of guts.

In fact, the actual existence of the tantien and the meridian system in general have long been debated by martial artists, chi kung practitioners, physicians, and scientists. The former two groups know from personal experience that chi is real and can be built up in the tantien and then propelled through the body, even though physicians and scientists state that there is no physiological basis for the tantien or the meridians.

So I was pretty much at loose ends for a couple of years until I noticed the headline of an article online that read something like: "Scientist Discovers Second Brain in the Gut." I saw that headline and instantly knew what it portended. And when I read the article about Gershon's research, I was sure I was on to something. I read the book, and it confirmed my suspicions. Gershon, even if he didn't know it, had discovered one of Taiji's most elusive truths: the physical reality and mechanism of the tantien.

I'm not going to go much into the specific content of the book except to say that if you think you might be put off by reading three hundred pages on a series of scientific discoveries about the stomach, intestines and neurotransmitters, you might be wrong. This isn't some dry scientific treatise but an engaging read that's a journey of discovery enhanced by the pacing of a whodunit. And

Gershon is a pretty funny writer, making this all the more enjoyable to read.

As if the information contained isn't interesting enough on its own. In an age when politicians and just about everybody else spout nothing but nonsense, lies, and obfuscation to the public, it's refreshing to follow the trail of an important scientific discovery and learn a lot of genuinely interesting and practical information along the way. You might know, for example, why politicians make you sick, but do you know why antidepressants cause nausea in the user? Gershon will tell you.

As for the practitioner of Taiji, Gershon's discoveries have a high degree of relevance in scientifically affirming the physiological structures and functional operation of the Conception Vessel, that elusive half of the Microcosmic Orbit. The information contained in his and Becker's books enabled me to synthesize a theory of what chi is, how it is generated in the tantien, what the meridians actually are, and how chi is propelled through them, as I detail in *The Wellspring*. I think it's a pretty sound theory, and I have Gershon and Becker to thank for providing a scientific basis to further my ideas and lend them a more solid stance.

The Electrical Activity of the Nervous System
A Textbook for Students

By Mary A. B. Brazier

It might seem strange to review a textbook on the nervous system in a survey of martial arts literature, but there is method to this madness. Obviously, the functioning of the nervous system should be of concern to all martial artists, and most should have a basic understanding of it. Hence this review of *The Electrical Activity of the Nervous System*, which I consider a companion piece to *The Body Electric*, by Robert O. Becker, and *The Second Brain*, by Michael D. Gershon, both reviewed above and both of which contain major discoveries about the bioelectromagnetic nature of the meridian system.

In writing about the nervous system, Brazier knows whereof she speaks. Born in England in 1904 to Quaker parents, she earned a Ph.D. in physiology and biochemistry in 1930, and began researching neuroscience at the Maudsley Hospital, London.[1] Ten years later, she moved to the United States on a Rockefeller Fellowship and taught and did research at the Massachusetts General Hospital, Harvard University, and the Massachusetts Institute of Technology for twenty years. Then she moved to the Brain Research Institute at UCLA, where she remained until her retirement. By then, she was internationally known as an outstanding neuroscientist, historian, author, and editor, with more than 250 books and articles to her credit.

There is a big difference, however, between her book and those by Becker and Gershon. They were writing for the general reader, while Brazier was writing a textbook for the advanced students of physiology and neuroscience of her day. While Becker and Gershon provide a sort of macro view of the two elements of the Microcosmic Orbit—the Governing and Conception Vessels, respectively—Brazier peers more deeply into the functioning of the nervous system at a micro level. The kind of work she was doing helped make it possible for Becker and Gershon to propose their theories about the electromagnetic nerve functioning of the spine/brain and the digestive tract, where chi is generated.

As this is a textbook, it isn't really amenable to review except to say that Brazier, as might be expected, covers her ground expertly. It is well written and has a number of illustrations and charts to aid in comprehension. If you want some basic knowledge of the nervous system or its constituent parts, this book would be a good place to start.

Notes
1 "Mary Brazier." *Wikipedia*, https://en.wikipedia.org/wiki/Mary_Brazier

Chinese Martial Arts Training Manuals
A Historical Survey

By Brian Kennedy and Elizabeth Guo
(Blue Snake Books, 2005, 328 pages)

Why the heck didn't I find out about this book when it was first published? But at least now I have. *Chinese Martial Arts Training Manuals: A Historical Survey*, by Brian Kennedy and Elizabeth Guo, is a martial arts bibliophile's dream: a knowledgeable, well-researched, interesting, clarifying, and highly readable survey of major martial arts manuals published in China during the flourishing of such books, mostly during the Chinese Republican era. It covers a number of aspects of kung fu history not found in other translated or English-language martial arts books as well as introduces a large number of Chinese martial arts authors whose works were significant and whose influence on kung fu literature proved lasting.

Here are the authors' bios from the back cover:

> Brian Kennedy, an attorney, has practiced Chinese martial arts since 1976. His previous books, published in Chinese, include *Witness Examination Skills* and *American Legal Ethics.*
>
> Elizabeth Nai-Jia Guo is a professional translator and practitioner of qi gong and hatha yoga. She has translated a wide

range of books into Chinese, including titles on church architecture, the history of science, and criminal law.

Together, Kennedy and Guo write a regular column for the magazine *Classical Fighting Arts*. They are also the editors of *Jingwu: The School that Transformed Kung Fu* (Blue Snake Books, 2010).

The book under consideration is divided into two parts. Part one covers the broad historical background of Chinese martial arts in general and martial arts literature specifically, while part two provides thumbnail bios of more than thirty authors/editors and short synopses of some of their books—often more than one. Both parts are of approximately equal length, and though neither is exhaustive, both are thorough enough. In their preface, the authors state:

> A word should be said about how the two co-authors shared the work. Brian Kennedy was primarily responsible for penning the first half, so the opinions, analysis, and ideas are his and are not necessarily shared by Elizabeth Guo, who was principal author of the second half of this work. The translations and the synopses of the books are largely her work.

We'll start our survey with Kennedy's half. He begins with an introduction that lays out the backstory and sources for Chinese martial arts training manuals. While one might expect these books to be valuable collector's items—and some are in their original publication—Kennedy cites Lion Books Martial Arts Publishing Company, a Taiwanese publisher of martial arts and health books, as a good source for reprints. I'll also discuss *Brennan Translations*, another excellent source for translations of such material, near the end of this review.

Kennedy then delves into that deepest and most mysterious of subjects: the historical sources for the martial arts in general and Chinese martial arts specifically. This entails a broad-ranging view that encompasses not only the hundreds of kung fu styles that have existed, but their relationships to the martial arts of other countries. Part and parcel of this is the methodology of martial arts practice, which almost always entails form work but also can incorporate a vast array of other aspects, such as ancillary exercises, chi kung, weapons, and herbal remedies. To get across his ideas, Kennedy utilizes hearty examples from martial arts history, doing his best to stay within the parameters of the real rather than the legendary or the hyperbolic.

To be clear, though, Kennedy is not trying to relate a complete history of kung fu. Instead, he is using the general history of the art of kung fu as a rack to hang his reflections on the familial, social, and cultural aspects of kung fu practice and literature. Included is the distinction between internal and external styles and how their training methods are necessarily divergent. The material here is excellent and very well researched, and it gives a perspective on the development of the Chinese martial arts that even the Chinese seem to have lost in the welter of legend, hyperbole, lies, and cinematic kung fu mayhem.

I tend to be wary of kung fu histories since so many of them are littered with error, deliberate as well as unintentional and received, but the more I read about it, the stronger the outlines become, sort of like a shape materializing but not quite fully emerged from a fog. In this respect, Kennedy's shape seems more distinct than many others, principally because he does not rely solely on historical "facts," which always are suspect regarding martial arts history, to inform his overview. Rather, he leans on the social, cultural, and political milieus prevalent in different parts of China and Taiwan during their lengthy and diverse histories. These elements characterize his history as much as they inform it.

Any overview of kung fu must, of course, include a discussion of chi/qi, to which Kennedy devotes five pages. His history begins with a caveat from Henry Ford: "History is more or less bunk." Kennedy extends this sentiment to kung fu literature, and he does expose the bunk—inconsistencies, biases, exaggerations, and pure fabrications—and his reasons are sound and well stated. He is a lawyer, after all. For example, he examines the fantastical tales that arose around Sun Lutang, such as Sun being able to pace a galloping horse, and determines that these tales did not originate with Sun but "were the invention of students, friends, or journalists looking for exciting copy." Kennedy prefers to concentrate on those authors and manuals that don't just purport to give the "real stuff" but actually do so, and Sun and his five works are among them.

Next, Kennedy looks at martial arts historians, beginning with Tang Hao, a martial artist who lived part of his life as a wanted man, not because of criminality but because of politics. Of Tang, Kennedy writes:

> The life of Tang Hao (1897–1959) is worth recounting in some detail. There are three reasons for this: first, he was quite influential. He is viewed as being the greatest Chinese martial arts historian that ever lived. Second, many of his comments and criticisms regarding martial arts history and martial arts writing are still valid today. third, he led an interesting, exciting life. [See the list below for the titles of Tang's writings discussed by the authors.]

In his description of Tang—and throughout the first section—Kennedy intersperses details, factoids, anecdotes, and definitions as well as background information and a critical analysis, all economically but interestingly stated. You'll have to read the book to learn about Tang, but to whet your appetite, I'll just say that Tang does not give credit to either Bodhidharma or Chang Sanfeng for knowing or creating Shaolin or Taiji, respectively. Kennedy writes:

> Not surprisingly, Tang Hao made a fair number of enemies, including authors of such books [that gave credit to Bodhidharma and Chang].

As an example of how Kennedy weaves historical information seamlessly into his narrative, he uses the fact that Tang was physically threatened to examine the familial structure of martial arts schools, in which disciples literally became members of the teacher's family and formed a kung fu brotherhood that stood in defense not just of its organization and teacher, but of its individual members.

Following the section on Tang Hao, which occupies twenty-two pages, come much shorter bios of five other important kung fu historians, each including the titles of some of their more significant works. After this, Kennedy presents a chapter titled, "Westerners Researching Chinese Martial Arts History." He leads off this chapter with thumbnail bios of several Westerners who were seminal influences in the dissemination of kung fu to the Western world. First is

Robert W. Smith, and no wonder. Smith's books were often the first in English to describe several specific Chinese martial arts, and his influence was significant. Others mentioned in the chapter are Dan Miller, Jarek Szymanski, Stanley E. Henning, Douglas Wile, and Andrea Faulk. He is careful to say that these aren't the only examples—Donn Draeger and Tim Cartmell readily come to mind, but to be fair, Cartmell is frequently mentioned throughout the book.

The birthplaces of Chinese martial arts are treated in the next chapter. The Shaolin and Wudang connections are examined, as well as several other locations. Unsurprisingly, the author is not impressed with the standard stories of Bodhidharma and Chang San-feng, and he essays a more rational approach to kung fu's genesis. Many of the ideas he presents will be familiar to readers of martial arts literature, and I leave it to you to judge Kennedy's accuracy. While I love the mythic genesis stories, I think that historians like Kennedy and those mentioned above often provide more informed and detailed accounts possessing greater veracity.

Kennedy covers Chinese martial arts classification schemes next: internal/external, northern/southern, and Shaolin/Wudang. None, he says, are very accurate. He also states that such distinctions "are all of fairly recent vintage, and they all generate controversy whenever they are used." However, he concludes, they are of "somewhat helpful in finding one's way around the multitude of systems that make up Chinese martial arts." He covers internal/external first, which entails a further classification system: hard/soft. The distinctions here are that internal styles rely on intrinsic energy (chi, perhaps) and focus on defense (generally), while external styles rely more on strength and speed and focus on offense. He concludes this section with:

> It is worth noting, too, that the internal–external classification scheme is of recent vintage, first being used in the late Qing and Republican period.

The northern/southern scheme, he says, refers primarily to Shaolin systems, with the division being defined by: Northern Legs, Southern Fist. Northern styles feature more kicking, and southern styles more handwork. The Shaolin/Wudang classification is a sort of mix between the two schemes described above that relies on the supposed location of the genesis of the arts broken down this way. Any martial art that is not specifically Wudang is Shaolin.

> This classification scheme is long on romance and short on reality. While it is true that the Wudang Mountains were home to a great number of Taoist temples, it is equally true that none of the three Wudang martial arts were invented there.... This classification scheme was first used by the National Guoshu Academy in the 1920s.

A discussion of religion and morality in relation to the martial arts is featured next.

> The idea that martial arts were linked with either Taoist or Buddhist philosophy came about when martial arts stopped being a practical trade and started to be a form of recreation for the upper and middle classes. This process began in the late 1800s and accelerated at the start of the Republican era (1912).

This interesting section shows that the move of martial arts away from traditional forms toward fighting forms (mixed martial arts, for example) is, in a sense, simply a return to the practical aspects of the martial arts for a practical era. But it also shows that mixed martial arts don't just take the best of moves that work well in combat and mix them up, no matter where they came from. It demonstrates that the martial arts can, and have, absorbed a great deal of social, cultural, and spiritual aspects from all the cultures they have entered into through the centuries.

The following chapter is devoted to the Imperial military examinations prevalent during the Republican era. As the dynasties of the past died and a new form of government was rising, some of the older ways that martial artists made a living—teaching, fighting in tournaments, or serving as physicians, street entertainers, or criminals—began vanishing, leaving the military as the predominant career path for martial artists. For those who are interested, Kennedy goes into some detail on the parameters of these examinations.

Next is short chapter that basically is a list of the top twelve Chinese martial arts classics as formulated by Professor Kang Ge Wu in his *The Complete Practical Book of Chinese Martial Arts*, and this leads into a chapter that discusses the history of Chinese martial arts training manuals. This begins with the Legendary period, moves on to the Early Woodblock period, the Hand-copied period, and the Republican period, and winds up in the modern era. These categories might be self-explanatory, but Kennedy delves at length into each one, divulging a number of interesting details as well as clearly laying out the overarching progression of the development of these manuals in conjunction with the historical, social, and cultural changes taking place in China.

The following chapter is titled "Authorship, Various Editions, Content of Training Manuals, and the Audience." It examines all the aspects of a book or manual not strictly related to specific content. Prominent authors are highlighted, but Kennedy begins with the problem of ascertaining actual authorship of kung fu training manuals. Only part of the problem is that some of the authors of such manuals concealed their true identities behind the personae of "historical progenitors" of their martial arts. An excellent example of this, Kennedy says, is Wu Yuxiang, one of the top students of both the Chen and Yang families and founder of Wu/Hao style Taiji. After all, it seems quite convenient that *The Salt Shop Manual* containing Wang Tseung-yueh's *Taiji Classics* was almost too fortuitously discovered in a salt shop owned by Wu's brother.

Other difficulties are that some manuals involved the hands of too many authors and editors to determine exactly who was responsible for what. Sometimes uncredited books from the past were passed on with contributions by unnamed persons, and even some single authors remained entirely unnamed or their names invoke no historical background on them. Surveys of works of these several types can be found in co-author Guo's Part II of the book.

As might be surmised from the above, Kennedy asserts in a section on different editions:

> The vast majority of books mentioned in this survey have had an original publication followed with re-publication in multiple forms from multiple publisher with or without the original author's or publisher's consent. Copyright is largely a Western concept.

The general content of these manuals begins with a quote from Liu Kang Yi, a respected Taiwanese martial arts historian and publisher, who said, "They are all the same manual." It is an amusing insight that largely bears out, as I can attest after reading hundreds of martial arts books and manuals and reviewing them all in this series, including many from the eras covered by Kennedy and Guo.

But Liu's observation, while generally apt, is not completely true. The modern era has seen the production of perhaps thousands of similar manuals, but also scores of martial arts books that break the norm in one way or another, whether by focusing on history or specific techniques or some other aspect beyond functional training in a form or weapon play. And such more-in-depth books existed even in the Republican period, such as Xiang Kairan's *My Experience of Practicing Taiji Boxing*. (This very interesting book is not mentioned in the book now under review, but you can read about it in Volume V of this series.) Xiang's book is definitely not the same as the norm, and it wasn't the only one. But Kennedy presents the basic structure that most of these manuals take.

There is a brief discussions of the artistic aspects of training manuals, and indeed, illustrations and photos abound in both sections, reproduced from the manuals under discussion, to give the reader a sense of the development of the art of the genre. Kennedy then discusses the target audience for these manuals—or more properly, audiences, for the audience changed over time, from predominantly the military, to literate upper-class civilians, and finally to the middle-class. The author then devotes a short chapter to Liu Kang Yi, a Taiwanese collector of Chinese martial arts training manuals and founder of Lion Books Martial Arts Publishing. Liu's goal is "to preserve martial arts culture through high-quality reprints of such older Chinese martial arts training manuals." Kennedy states that Liu's collection contains two thousand out-of-print manuals and five hundred more from the Republican era.

Kennedy devotes the next chapter to issues surrounding translation. Just about every translator I've read—and that's a lot by now—issues similar caveats about the ability—or rather inability—of a translation to be both literally accurate and artistically sound. It's kind of like the problems physicists have with sub-atomic structure, for a photon can be viewed as a wave or as a point, but not both at the same time. Frequent readers of martial arts translations undoubtedly have encountered these sorts of caveats, but to Kennedy's credit, his explanation is both more detailed and explanatory beyond the obvious truism that certain words and concepts in any language can be fraught with such an excess of meanings that accurate literal translation is completely impossible.

A chapter on how Chinese martial artists made their livings over time is next, and the short answer is as soldiers, law enforcement personnel, physicians, opera troupers and street performers, security personnel and bodyguards, or criminals—sometimes a measure of more than one of these. The author gives a fine breakdown of most of these types and their prevalence during certain periods of Chinese history. And he weaves in historical features that abounded in popular culture. One story concerns the association between Chinese opera troupes and Hung Gar Shaolin masters who were on the run from Qing forces after escaping the massacre at the Shaolin Temple, which had been masterminded by the treacherous and evil monk, Bai Mai. (Or so the story goes.)

Next, the author relates the history of the martial arts in Taiwan, which became the de facto repository of Chinese martial arts during their decades of suppression in mainland China. He takes this history from the 1100s, when Chinese settlement of the island really began, supplanting the indigenous Hakka people who were the original immigrants from China centuries earlier. Then he moves rapidly through several succeeding waves of immigration to 1621, each one bringing with it various styles of martial arts.

The chapter then discusses Qing-era martial arts in Taiwan and how they were taught, important manuals of the time, militias, important kung fu centers, styles, and the Japanese era, digressing at each turn to explain the progression, divulge facts, and relate anecdotes. One of the longest and most entertaining is about Liao Tien Ding, the Righteous Thief of Taiwan. Described by the author as melding of Robin Hood and Billy the Kid, but using kung fu instead of arrows or bullets, Liao was a folk hero in his country for attacking and robbing the rich and the police. He was said to have had "burglary kung fu."

Sections on politics and the martial arts and important modern figures follow, and Kennedy points out that a few of these individuals were profiled in Robert W. Smith's *Chinese Boxing: Masters and Methods*. (See Volume III of this series for a review.)

And that concludes Kennedy's contributions. Part II of the book, written by Elizabeth Guo, profiles more than thirty authors/editors and surveys their more important works. I would characterize Guo's reviews as far sketchier than mine in terms of depth of survey and criticism, but they are much heavier on the historical background. Certainly, being Taiwanese, fluent in Chinese, and a researcher with a large number of primary resources within her grasp give depth and veracity to her profiles and surveys. At the very least, she opens the door on significant works and what their publication meant in a larger cultural context as well as to martial arts literary history.

Each several-page chapter covers a single author, or occasionally multiple authors and/or editors. Some cover only a single work, some several. Each gives, to one degree or another, a concise but fairly in-depth historical background on the author, his art, and the genesis of the book in addition to a thumbnail survey of contents. These reviews aren't a critical response. After all, according to the authors, these all are topnotch or otherwise significant examples of the kung fu authors' arts—literary as well as martial. Instead they serve to give a basis for critical evaluation and as bait to lure your interest.

I'm not going to try to describe each author Guo discusses. That's her job, and she does it ably. But I will mention a few. The first profile is of *New Book on Effective Military Techniques* by General Qi Jiguang (1528–1587). A complete translation with commentary of this book can be found in Dan Docherty's *Tai Chi Chuan: Decoding the Classics for the Modern Martial Artist*. (Reviewed in Volume V of this series.) The next one is Sun Lutang, whose five books on the internal martial arts were groundbreaking and influential across the entire genre of martial arts literature and elevated his reputation among internal stylists.

Most of the manuals Gou cites display and discuss open-hand and weapons forms across a number of systems and styles, but there are notable exceptions, such as *Shanghai City Police Training Center's Rope Techniques for Arrest*, which discusses and illustrates ways to use rope to efficiently and effectively bind prisoners in ways that serve anywhere between handcuffs and a straightjacket. There also is *Western Boxing*, an English book translated into Chinese without the translator mentioning the original author's name. (I'd like to take a look at a translation of this one to see if the publisher stole the first half of *Western Boxing and World Wrestling* by John F. Gilbey [Robert W. Smith], reviewed in Volume I of this series.)

Guo's section is followed by a glossary and a helpful index. If the book lacks anything it is a complete bibliography to aid the reader in doing further research and reading. However, I went through the book and compiled a list of all the authors and works that Guo and Kennedy profile. (See below.) Note that this list includes not just the thirty-odd authors of Guo's section, but also all the ones Kennedy discussed or mentioned in his section. This will give you an excellent idea of who and what to look for should you be interested in reading some of the manuals yourself.

On that note, I have to mention *Brennan Translations*, a website on which translator Paul Brennan has posted translations of so many Chinese martial arts books that I've lost count. Even better, they primarily are the same sorts of books discussed by Kennedy and Guo. In fact, at least fifty of the books he reviews are either specifically named in *Chinese Martial Arts Training Manuals* or are by authors who are mentioned. So Brennan's site is an extremely important resource for those interested in this sort of material. (https://brennantranslation.wordpress.com) (See below for a more thorough look at *Brennan Translations*.)

Kennedy and Guo's book is just the sort of reference work to appeal to a bibliophile like me. It might not be encyclopedic, but it has much to say about the history of Chinese martial arts manuals, their development, and why they were important, both as a genre and as specific examples. And the way the authors weave the warp of kung fu into the woof of history yields a tapestry both interesting and artful.

As I said in my opening, I wish I'd known about this book when it first appeared. But now that I know it does, I imagine it will not be read this once, shelved, and never read again (by me), but will be picked over again and again as I read more examples of the manuals it discusses and turn to writing reviews of them. Kudos to the authors for a book not just well conceived and well done but much needed.

Authors and Works Discussed in *Chinese Martial Arts Training Manuals*

For those who wish to read translations of these manuals for themselves, many of them can be found on *Brennan Translations* (https://brennantranslation.wordpress.com).

Key:
* Translations that are available from *Brennan Translations* (as of the latest publication of this book).
( ) Titles used by translator Paul Brennan.
[ ] Titles by named authors that are not included in *Chinese Martial Arts Training Manuals* but that appear in *Brennan Translations*.

Bodhidharma (attributed)
    The Muscle Change Classic
    The Tendon Change Classic
    Washing Bone Marrow Classic
Chang Nai Zhou
    The Book of Chang Style Martial Techniques
Chen Ting Rui (trans. & commentary)
    Western Boxing
Chen Wei Ming (Chen Weiming)
    [Additional Photos for the Taiji Boxing Solo Set] *
    [Bagua Palming and Qinna Photos] *
    Taijiquan (The Art of Taiji Boxing) *
    Taiji Sword (Yang Style Taiji Sword) *
    Taijiquan Questions and Answers (Answering Questions about Taiji) *
Chen Zi Ming (Chen Ziming)
    Chen Family Taijiquan Passed Through Generations (The Inherited Chen Family Taiji boxing Art) *
Cheng Zong You
    On Martial Arts During the Fallow Season
Chou Chi Chun
He Liang Chen
    Notes of Battle Arrays

Huang Bai Jia (Huang Baijia)
   Internal Boxing Method (Boxing Methods of the Internal School) *
Huang Bao Ing
   Shun Hand Boxing
Huang Bo Nien
   Xingyi Fist and Weapons Instruction
   Dragon Body Bagua
Huang Wen Shu
   The Essence of Yang Style Taijiquan (The Skills and Essentials of Yang Style Taiji Boxing) *
   Miscellaneous Talks on Martial Arts (Martial Arts Discussions) *
Jiang Rong Qiao (Jiang Rongqiao)
   Xingyi Mother Fists
   Mizongquan
   Rare Bagua Spear
   Tiger Tail Whip
   Qing Ping Sword
   Kun Wu Sword (Kunwu Sword Neigong) *
   Shaolin Staff (An Authentic Description of Shaolin Staff Methods) *
   [The Taiji Manual of Yao Fuchun & Jiang Rongqiao] *
Jin Ing Zhong (Jin Enzhong)
   Shaolin 72 Arts Practice Method
   Martial Arts Who's Who
   Illustrated Original One Qi Gong
   [Saber Manual] *
Jin Yi Ming (Jin Yiming)
   The Basics of Boxing
   [Dragon Shape Sword] *
   [Teachings of Jin Jiafu, recorded by Jin Yiming] *
   [Single Defense Saber] *
Kang Ge Wu
   The Compete Practical Book of Chinese Martial Arts

Lam Sai Wing
> Taming the Tiger Fist
> Tiger and Crane Fist
> Iron Thread Form

Li Cun Yi
> Yue Fei's Intent Boxing (Xingyi's Five Elements—Combined Volume: Five Elements Manual/Continuous Boxing Manual?) *

Li Jing Lin (source material)

Huang Yuan Xiou (ed)
> The Main Points of Wudang Sword

Li Xian Wu (Li Xianwu)
> Taijiquan (Taiji Boxing) *

Liu Jin Sheng

Zhao Jiang
> Chin Na Methods

Ma Ming Da

Matsuda Ryuchi
> An Illustrated History of Chinese Martial Arts *

Morris, Andrew D.
> Marrow of a Nation: A History of Sport and Physical Culture in Republican China

Qi Ji-Guang, General
> New Book of Effective Military Techniques (Qi Jiguang's Boxing Classic. Chapter 14, Archery Principles Chapter 13) *

Ren Zhi Cheng

Gao Zhi Kai
> Study of Yin–Yang Eight Coiling Palms (A response to Sun Xi Kun's The Real Teaching of Bagua Quan)

Shanghai City Police Training Center
> Rope Techniques for Arrest

Sun Fuquan (Sun Lutang)
> The Study of Xingyi Boxing (The Xingyi Manual of Sun Lutang) *
> The Study of Bagua Boxing (The Bagual Manual of Sun Lutang) *
> The Study of Taiji Boxing (The Taiji Manual of Sun Lutang) *
> The True Essence of Boxing (Further Writings of Sun Lutang) *
> The Study of Bagua Sword (Bagua Sword) *
> [The Voices of Sun Lutang's Teachers] *

Sun Xi Kun
    The Real Teaching of Bagua Quan
Tang Hao
    Taiji Boxing and Neijia Boxing
    A Study of Shaolin and Wudang
    Neijia Boxing
    The Qi Qi Fist Classic
    A Study of Chinese Martial Arts Illustrations
    Wong Wugong Taiji Linking Saber
    Wong Song Lance Manual
    The Lost Old Chinese Sword Method
    Essays of Hsinjen Residence
    Series on Qing Dynasty Archery
    A Study of Chinese Sports Illustrations
    A Study of "Secrets of Shaolin Boxing"
    Studies of the Emei School of Boxing
Tang Ji Ren (ed. & compiler)
    Tang Family External Big Hong Fist *
    Tang Shun Zhi
    Martial Book/Martial Arts Collection *
Tong Zhong Yi
    Chinese Wrestling *
Unknown/Various
    Seven Books of Martial Arts Classics *
    Six Harmonies Boxing Manual (edited by Tang Hao) *
Wan Lai Sheng (Wan Laisheng)
    The Common Basis of Martial Arts *
    A Collection of Reviews on Martial Arts *
    [On Silent Meditation] *
    [Original Postures of Taiji Boxing Explained] *
Wang Xian Bin
    A Detailed Explanation of Intent Qi Gong *
Wu Shu
    Record of Arms *
Wu Wen Han
    The Complete Book of the Essence and Applications of Wu Style Taijiquan *

Wu Yu Xing
  Taijiquan Classic (Attributed to Wang Tseung-Yueh *
Xie Dien, Gao Zhi Jen, Chiang Xin Shan (eds.)
  Xingyi Training Materials *
  The Essence of Form Imitating Fist (Xie) *
Xu Yi Qian (Xu Yiqian)
  Chuan Na Quan *
  [Illustrated Sancai Sword] *
[A Newly Arranged Handbook for the Footwork-Training Set] *
Xu Yu Xin
  Fist Methods Study Textbook *
Xu Zhen
  The Authentication of Taijiquan Training Manuals *
  The Study of the Authentication of Taijiquan *
  The Study of Illustrations of Original Methods of Shaolin *
  A Survey of National Martial Arts *
Xuan Ji (Shaolin Monk—original author)
Zhang Ming E, Zhang King Zhao, Cao Huan Dou (eds)
  Fist Classic; Fist Method *
Yang De Hua
  Wall-Breaking Shaolin (aka. Bagua Palm Method) *
Yang Kui Yuan
  Complete Book of Guoshu *
Yin Yu Zhang (Yin Yuzhang)
  Slashing Saber Practice (Practice Methods for Cleaving Saber Techniques) *
  A Brief Book of Baguazhang (A Concise Book of Bagua Palming) *
Yu Da You
Zheng Qi Hall Anthology
Zhu Xia Tian (Zhu Xiatian)
  Boxing Book *
  [Midnight Style Lohan Boxing Illustrated] *
  [Secret Teachings of Chinese Martial Arts: Shaolin Mountain-Guarding Midnight Style-Lohan Boxing Illustrated]*

Not Lost in Translation
Brennan Translations

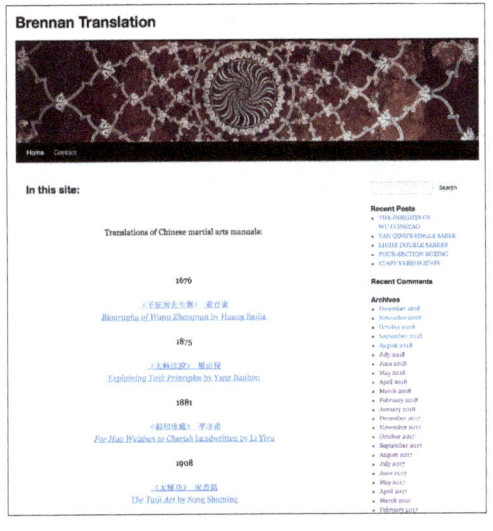

Most practitioners of the martial arts fall into the beginner to intermediate levels, while some rise even higher in their respective arts, from skillfulness to mastery. And then there are those rarities: prodigies who reach the absolute pinnacle of achievement and beyond.

So it is, also, with martial arts literature. Martial arts authors, from the mediocre to the pedestrian to the competent if not gifted, abound—I'm speaking here about the quality of the literature, not the martial expertise of the authors. It seems as if many martial artists who have reached a certain level of competency want to write a book or two on their art. It's almost like a rite of passage, and no wonder, for writing about a martial art forces the author to examine, re-examine, and more deeply examine the art in question, thereby lending a further learning experience to one's study that can be quite enlightening. I am guilty of this, myself. I think my books are pretty good, but I recognize that there are numerous authors whose experience, depth of understanding, and ability to communicate the ideas and principles underlying their arts far outshine mine. They are like the guiding stars of the heavens.

Until now, I have largely confined my reviews to authors and their original books, but I also have recognized the efforts of several authors who have been notable translators into English of works on Taiji and other martial arts. Yang Jwing-Ming, Douglas Wile, and Stuart Alve Olson, among others, come readily to mind. But no matter how luminous the efforts of these translators, they can't hold a candle to Paul Brennan, one of those bright, guiding stars within Taiji literature. Welcome to *Brennan Translations*, where, since February 2011, Brennan has been posting translations of Chinese martial arts books and manuals.

Although the earliest text in Brennan's blog is about 340 years old, it is a notable exception. Most of the original works Brennan tackles are from China's Republican era (1912–1949), which I tend to refer to as the Neo-Classical era of Chinese martial arts literature. I've personally witnessed the inception, burgeoning, and development of martial arts literature in English, and the plethora of books on Taiji and other martial arts is almost boggling after just fifty years. Apparently, Chinese martial artists through the ages have not been immune to the impulse to author books. Imagining the number of martial arts books and manuals available in English is difficult, but developing a tally of Chinese martial arts books and manuals is impossible. If you count time from the Yellow Emperor (Huang Ti) who lived circa 2700 BC and wrote treatises on Chinese medicine and martial arts, the Chinese have been writing such stuff about ninety-five times as long as writers in English have.

I don't know if Brennan realizes how daunting his task is—or if he even cares. He just seems to be intent on making as big a dent as possible in the mountain of literature looming before him. Apparently he doesn't grant interviews, which doesn't do much to dispel a vision of him as a translating cyborg operating at a fantastic pace, though he did tell me a few facts about his blog. Toward the beginning of his efforts, several months might have passed between postings, but since 2013, he's posted one translation almost every month, and sometimes two or three works at the same time. This is no mean feat. Many of the originals of these works can be described as being pamphlets or booklets, but just as many are full-length works, some logging two to three hundred pages.

Remarkably for a martial arts reading public accustomed to paying for published translations, Brennan's translations are available free on his website. They are in blog form only, and can be read online or printed off the website. He writes:

Although there are apparently some pdfs of several of these things floating around online, they were made and shared without my permission. I give no pdf option in the site itself. The reason I do not supply downloadable pdfs or make paper publications of these translations is because I often make adjustments and corrections to them. Every new book I work on gives me insights into the ones I have finished. Thus I find it better to simply direct people to the site itself so they will always have access to the updated versions.

Free doesn't necessarily mean good. In one sense of this, many of the books and manuals Brennan translates are no more informative than the common books or manuals by some of today's modern authors. There are exceptions notable for being either really informative or for being written by historically significant authors—Sun Lutang, for example—but even the less adept or less significant books among these translations provide a wide variety of viewpoints and approaches to the arts they discuss, bringing in each author's individual understandings and ways of expressing ideas. Put differently, even a mid-level author can drop a piece of information in such a way that it triggers understanding and advancement in the reader. In addition to being products of a culture in transition over a span of several centuries, these books likewise display an intrinsic historical view of the development of the martial arts during that time. It is significant, then, that Brennan is making them available to those of us who do not read Chinese.

That brings us to the second sense of the idea that free is not necessarily good. One might suspect that the quality of Brennan's work is not high, particularly considering his considerable output. I don't speak or read Chinese, so I can't personally compare his translations to the originals, but others have. Violet Li of the *Tai Chi Examiner*[1] explains that many of the older originals were written in "wenyan wen," or Classical Chinese, which was very formal, economical, poetic, and difficult to comprehend. Nevertheless, she says, Brennan does a good job of translating without loss of meaning. I can personally judge, however, the quality of the finished product in terms of grammar, diction, flow, and so forth, and I can say that Brennan seems to be competent at the very least, and usually excellent.

His translations appear to be straightforward iterations of their originals without the sort of explanations and commentary that someone like Yang Jwing-ming might append to the text. Such commentary can vastly amplify the meaning of the content, but for anyone interested in just taking in the originals, Brennan has the goods. He does offer occasional historical commentary, however. When the original text alludes to some historical event or has some other reference that the average Western reader probably wouldn't know about, Brennan helpfully provides a bit of information to enrich the reader's understanding of the backstory.

Brennan's methodology is familiar and used by many translators. He provides the original Chinese text, broken into paragraphs or passages, and follows each of those with its translation. He also includes scans of interior drawings and/or photos, so that the end product best represents the original publication. By his own reckoning, he provides scans of the books' covers only about half the time.

> I include scans of calligraphy that appear in the original books, which sometimes features on the cover. In those cases, the calligraphy is the focus, and the cover is just along for the ride.

Brennan's work covers many books that have been translated previously, and it also introduces the Western reading public to many more that have not—and probably would have remained that way if it wasn't for his efforts. I've reviewed his entire output up until the time I published this series, but he's still at work, cranking out translations as fast as I can read and review them. I was tempted to include a list of his work, to date, but I realized how futile that would be. He's constantly adding new material, and any list would soon be obsolete. You'll just have to go to his website to view his offerings, although I have provided cross-reference lists of the books he translates with mentions of the books or their authors in *Chinese Martial Arts Training Manuals*, by Brian Kennedy and Elizabeth Guo, reviewed above.

Brennan's offerings are indexed in several ways. In the main column, he highlights a number of works produce from 1676 to 1963. In the narrower right-hand column, he first lists a handful of his more recent posts. Below that is a much longer list of posting dates ranging, as of this writing, from February 2011 to July 2022. There is no information in this list about the contents of each post, which is something of a detriment since you have to open each one to see what's inside. You might find one translation there, or three. Grouped offerings often are works by a single author. Under this long list of posting dates, which keeps getting longer, is a shorter, more static list of six categories: The Complete Works of Sun Lutang, The Complete Works of Yin Qianhe, Shaolin, Taiji, Xingyi, and Uncategorized. Each of these links open up into its own mini-library.

The system of adding material under its posting date might have served the site adequately early on, but after twelve years of furious accretion, the list is getting pretty unwieldy. If I had a suggestion to Brennan, it would be to revise this list into three indexes: one by author, one by title, one by subject. The latter would be little more than a minor expansion of the shorter, six-item list that's already in place. There is a search feature, however, if you know what you're looking for, either by title or by author, though I've found it a little glitchy.

While Brennan provided me with some clarification about the site and its contents, you can forget about searching for information on the man himself. He'll have to remain the B. Traven or Thomas Pynchon of Taiji translators. The *Brennan Translations* site is bare bones, containing only the translations and the several ways they are indexed. Completely lacking is any information on Brennan himself. When Violet Li requested an interview to learn more about the site and his efforts, he declined, writing:

> The whole point of my translation blog is to allow the original authors to speak for themselves, and so to do them justice I ought to try to stay in the background.[1]

Okay, Mr. Brennan, we won't begrudge you. After all, your work speaks volumes.

Brennan Translations can be found at:
https://brennantranslation.wordpress.com

Notes

1 http://violetlitaichi.com/wp-content/uploads/2016/07/Paul-Brennan-is-God-sent-Examiner.com_.pdf

PART VI

Film & Television

Kung Fu
Cinema of Vengeance

By Verina Glaessner
(Bounty Books, 1974, 134 pages)

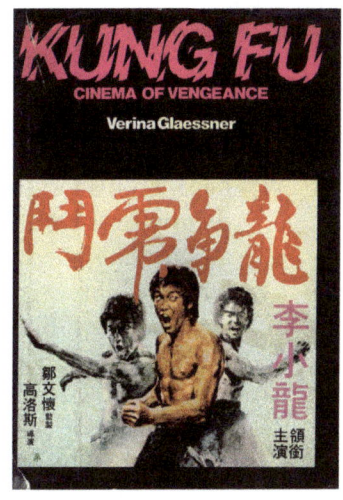

Back in the day—the early 1980s, that is—martial arts cinema was just coming into its own in the United States, and leading the pack was the output from Shaw Brothers Studio, Golden Harvest Productions, and a double-handful of independent film companies, most centered in Hong Kong. This output wasn't new, however, and American audiences who watched this fare on Saturday afternoon TV were seeing a genre already a decade in the making. Enter the chopsocky movie, the Wonton Western.

Verina Glaessner was on hand early enough to have developed an interest in the kung fu film as the publication date of this book attests. Most Westerners didn't see this stuff until years later unless they habituated Chinese cinemas in some of America's larger cities. With *Kung Fu: Cinema of Vengeance*, she summarizes the history of the martial art film—mostly in China but with some overlap with Japan—and discusses its development through different styles of filmmaking and periods of audience expectations. Her account ends around the time of Bruce Lee's death.

Chapter one is an overview of the kung fu film and its historical antecedents, taking the matter almost to the end of the era. Along the way, she addresses Chinese representation in American films, such as Fu Manchu, before moving on to discuss the environment—namely the city of Hong Kong—from which the films emerged and to which they contributed. She writes:

> Kung fu films are poverty row cinema, generally critically despised and berated for what is seen as their sensationalist concentration on violent action at the expense of such comfortable attributes as character development, nuance and even narrative tension.

"How would you define your audience?" she asks a Shaw Brothers employee. "There are a lot of poor people," is the reply, "a lot of illiterate people in Hong King... they go to the films."

The reasons for their attendance at Hong Kong's more than ninety theaters at the time was to escape their environment.

> Fifty-five percent of the population is under 25. A permanent land boom escalates rents. There is a serious drug addiction problem. Welfare provisions are inadequate. There is a high illiteracy rate and it is still permissible for parents to keep a child away from school if real financial need can be shown. A ten-hour day and a six-day week are usual. A reputable magazine estimated some ten percent of Hong King's gross national product to come from corrupt practices, mainly from the big three—gambling, prostitution and drugs. Not surprisingly, violent crime increased some 218 per cent between 1968 and 1972.

No wonder kung fu cinema was the vogue, no matter how bad the films were from a critical standpoint.

The next chapter covers the motifs of the kung fu film as opposed to those of Western cinema before moving on to the dichotomy between the spiritual and health-promoting aspects of the martial arts and their explicit violence. Following this, the author talks about several basic groupings or styles of martial arts: karate, Shaolin, Taekwondo, Taiji, and Wing Chun, and her descriptions, while basically accurate, are not deep.

"The Producers" is the next chapter, and it covers mainly the Shaw Brothers from their beginnings to well into the decay of the kung fu film. The way Shaw Brothers grew as a studio, the changing styles of the films they produced, and many of the actors who gave the studio clout are discussed. Raymond Chow, who worked for the Shaws before leaving to open his own studio, Golden Harvest, is similarly dealt with.

Directors and their action stars feature next, with Glaessner skimming through them like a drone flying over the landscape. And like that drone, it can pick out basic features, though the detail gets lost.

A chronology of the kung fu film occupies the following chapter. This history goes back to the 1930s but it focuses on the 1960s and 1970s. Again, the changing style of the movies over the course of those two decades is touched on—from sword-play films to rip-offs of James Bond films and other Western cinema to the chopsocky film as we know it.

After that, each of the next four chapters covers the career of a particular martial artist: Angela Mao, Bruce Lee, Wang Yu, and David Chiang. Oddly, Glaessner didn't seem to understand just how profoundly Bruce Lee altered the fundamental nature of the martial arts film—and even the nature of the martial arts as a whole—and she even states that he was not as important as some of the other stars she discusses.

The last chapter is titled, appropriately enough, "The Final Blow." In it, the author shows how the kung fu film deteriorated into pastiche, corn, horror, and porn. For her, that was the end of the genre.

Kung Fu: The Cinema of Vengeance was probably a lot more significant when it first appeared in the midst of the chopsocky explosion—even before the shock wave of that explosion reached Americans shores. One plus to her effort is that she managed to interview several highly placed individuals, including Run Run Shaw, head of Shaw Brothers, and Raymond Chow, head of Golden Harvest, to get their takes on how the kung fu movie developed out of earlier martial arts films—which China had produced since the Silent Era. She also obviously has seen many of the films since she writes about them with authority.

Unfortunately, that authority swims in the shallow end of the pool. Glaessner opts for scattershot renditions of movie plots instead of analysis to carry her through, and the results are both superficial and somewhat monotonous. After she's recited the plot of the fiftieth or sixtieth film, it all turns to mush. The writing tries to cover the lack of analysis with a sort of breathless rush from plot to plot that often places details here and there instead of combining them to dig deeper into what the plots—and the changing character of the films—might mean.

The book is replete with photos, most being black-and-white stills from frame shots, though there are eight pages of posters for some of the films, reproduced in full-color. But I also have a complaint about the stills, which are reproduced well enough. Almost all the stills are labeled simply with the name of the film it came from without naming the actors in the shot. This seems kind of lazy to me. Glaessner names many of the actors in the text, but it's often difficult to sync the names there with the faces in the photos.

In the end, *Kung Fu: The Cinema of Vengeance* reveals itself to be a lesser work that tantalizes more than it informs. See the next review for a more thorough look at the some of the same material.

Martial Arts Movies
From Bruce Lee to the Ninjas

By Richard Meyers, Amy Harlib, and Bill and Karen Palmer
(Citadel Press, 1985, 256 pages)

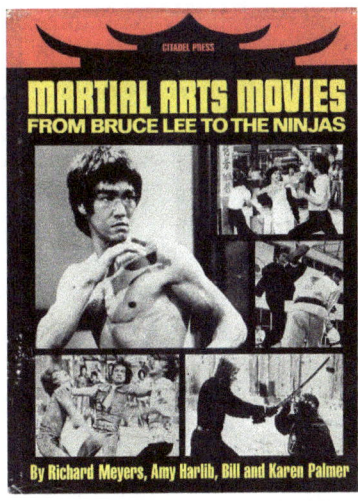

The subtitle of *Martial Arts Movies: From Bruce Lee to the Ninjas* describes the context of this book, which can be considered an extension of the history of martial arts cinema laid out in Verina Glaessner's *Kung Fu: Cinema of Vengeance*, which ended with Bruce Lee. (See review above.) Overall, though, *Martial Arts Movies* is a far superior book in depth, quality of analysis, and presentation.

In the introduction, the authors characterize the genre this way:

> We are a writer, a dancer, and two martial artists, but we all found common ground in Chinatown theaters, in exploitation movie houses, and on television, enjoying probably the most misunderstood, most underrated, and most vilified film genre ever projected. This reputation is not without its basis . At its worst, the martial ars movie is laughable, totally deserving of derision. But at its best, it can supply an audience exhilaration that cannot be found in any other cinema.

The intro goes on to say:

The best martial arts movies are period pieces in which people call upon their own greatest abilities to succeed, and not on cars to escape or on guns to win. The heroes of Oriental films are terrific acrobats and martial artists, magnificent athletes who can be literally breathtaking to watch. Their precision and power underline the attributes of the martial arts film.

The authors begin, as promised, with "Bruce Lee: The King of Kung Fu." It starts with a biography of Lee that does not stint in describing his sometimes volatile and somewhat harsh personality. But like the musician Robert Fripp once said, "Having an unpleasant personality is no impediment to success."

And succeed Lee did. Spectacularly, though it took a few years. The authors ably portray Lee from his rise to the flameout that ended his life, focusing on his twin careers of martial artist and film star. This is a good analysis of Lee and his career, and while it is an interesting account, it also is one that, forty years later, has been worked to death. But the controversies that remain around Lee's life, his skills, and his death still swirl, proving his importance to the genre.

Unfortunately, this is an importance the authors don't seem to grasp. Lee wasn't just a superlative martial artist and action star. In the span of only three and a half films, he singlehandedly punched and kicked the martial arts genre into a whole new paradigm by blending high-octane martial moves with a contemporary setting. Instead, the authors seem to consider him an outlier—a formidable martial artist, maybe, but not the game changer that he was.

But that's not to say that the chapter on Lee isn't interesting or that it doesn't highlight his many achievements. The inceptions of his films, their development, and Lee's co-stars all have a place in the account, which ends, of course, with his death.

Then the authors linger for a time on the spate of Bruce Lee clones that didn't so much explode onto the silver screen as they were simply flung at it to see what would stick. Not much did, and the authors excoriate most of their films—though not necessarily the stars themselves. This analysis might have been better stated had the authors a little prescience—or maybe simply better powers of observation. One Bruce Lee clone, Bruce Li (Ho Tsung Tao), for example, certainly wasn't Lee or much like him, but Li's kung fu was good and expressive and easy to comprehend. For me, watching martial arts movies isn't just about the thrill. It's an opportunity to see martial movements in action. A martial artist can learn much from watching screen fights, and Li's movements were clear and instructive.

And in an even greater instance of lack of prescience, the authors refer to Jet Lee (their spelling of Jet Li) as simply another Bruce Lee clone. Much to the contrary, Jet Li, while an admirer of and inspired by Bruce Lee, was to become one of literally a spare handful of kung fu stars to further propel the martial arts film into the 20th century.

But let's back off on the modernization for a moment, since the subtitle of this book—*From Bruce Lee to the Ninjas*, isn't entirely accurate. The next chapter, "China: The Source," dips back into Chinese and martial arts history to give a succinct account of the development of the martial arts from about 2500 BC, over the course of many dynasties to the present. Part of the purpose of this account is to relate historical events to the plots of the early kung fu movies produced by the Shaw Brothers and Golden Harvest Productions. It's a decent history that sets the stage for the plots and action to follow.

But before the action starts, the authors define a number of martial arts styles. These are all kung fu styles since the films of Japan are featured in a later chapter. The descriptions of the various styles are generally pretty good, though they don't include ones for Taiji, Bagua, or a couple of others, perhaps because those styles were not then well represented among the cinematic martial arts.

Next comes a history of the Chinese martial arts film, beginning with the earliest examples: *Thief in a Car* (1920s), *Monkey Fights Golden Leopard* (1926), and *The Burning of the Red Lotus Temple* (1929). More titles and tidbits about them lead the reader through the end of World War II. After that came Hu Peng's film series on the supposed life of Huang Fei Hung. I say supposed because little is known about the real Huang besides the facts that he was the son of one of the famous Ten Tigers of Kwangtung, he was a physician, and he was an expert in several forms of kung fu. But paucity of real-life factual material never stopped any writer or filmmaker, and Hu made an astounding eighty-five feature films about Huang over a twenty-year period. There weren't just a lot of them; this series became the foundation of the modern kung fu film.

The second important aspect of the martial arts film came to the fore in this series: a genuine kung fu expert was required to play the part. For the role of Huang, Hu chose Kwan Tai Hing, who seemed to delight in actually learning every esoteric kung fu skill Huang was reputed to have had and displaying them before the camera.

The authors dissect the Hu's Huang Fei Hung's films and their influence before moving on to the next chapter, which is on the chopsocky movies that emerged from Hong Kong in the early 1960s. They begin with *The One-Armed Swordsman*, starring Jimmy Wang in the title role. The film was a resounding success and launched the martial arts film into new territory. The authors write:

> After years of Confucian morality and bloodless, unconvincing, stagy fights, *The One-Armed Swordsman* showed them a tortured anti-hero who thought nothing of slaughtering his enemies.. And after all the abuse he had taken, the viewers went along with the slaughter—in fact, cheered it.

The film spawned two sequels of only slightly lesser quality, but it also paved the way for an avalanche of other films starring Wang, who became a superstar. The authors go through Wang's career, then look at the careers of David Chiang and Ti Lung, both familiar faces on the chopsocky screen. More martial arts actors are profiled, including Chen Kuan Tai, but all are part and parcel of the career of writer/director Chang Cheh, who made more than 200 martial arts films during his career.

Another high point is *The Water Margin*, which Chang produced in 1972. The U.S. title was *Seven Blows of the Dragon*, and while the authors state that the source material is Chi Naian's 14th-century novel, *Outlaws of the Marsh*, the book is more commonly known as *The Water Margin*. This is one heck of a book weighing in at just under 800 pages in the shorter version. This novel is justly considered the great-great grandfather of Wuxia, or, the martial arts adventure novel. Speaking of Chang, the authors write:

> He introduced a protracted-fight-scene filming style that has remained vital to this very day.

Remember, reader, "this very day" was back in the mid 1980s. Can you imagine how the authors would have reacted to the often protracted fight scenes in today's martial arts action movies? And another point. They make the same claim that many writers of prefaces to Chinese Republican Era martial arts manuals do: Guns spell the end of the martial arts and, in the opinion of the authors, the martial arts movie. After all, they reason, you can't fight guns with fists. The Boxer Rebellion proved that once and for all.

Their reasoning obviously didn't take into account that gunplay is, at base, just another martial art. Guns can be worked into plots that end in fights because, obviously, guns run out of ammo, and if the bad guy is still standing, the good guy has to take him out somehow.

More of Chang's movies are discussed, along with the martial artists he helped make stars of the genre, and the chapter ends by dissecting what the authors call Chang's masterpiece: 1982's *Five Elements Ninjas* (U.S. title, *Super Ninjas*).

The next important filmmaker the authors discuss is Liu Chia Liang.

> Only Liu Chia Liang seeks to make the greatest movies about the ancient arts of China without dilution or distortion. He exaggerates, he enlarges, certainly, but to him, kung fu is the thing. And it shows. He is without a doubt, and without peer, the finest pure martial arts movie maker.

Liu was, himself, a martial artists, having learned from his father, who learned from students of the real Huang Fei Hung. He began his film career as an actor but soon was behind the camera. His first movie, *The Spiritual Boxer*, was destined to lead the "new wave" of Chinese martial arts cinema, partly by adding humor and satire to deepen plots that formerly revolved mostly around revenge.

But that wasn't his only success. Among others is his 1978 *Thirty-Sixth Chamber of Shaolin* (U.S. title, *Master Killer*). This starred Liu's adopted brother, Liu Chia Hui, better known in the U.S. as Gordon Liu, who director Liu had used in a couple of previous films. What this film did was display the rigors of martial arts training and the determination, will power, and suffering necessary to achieve a high level. Gordon Liu's character is based on Liu Yu Te, a reluctant revolutionary who became the famous real-life monk, San-te.

> *Master Killer* was an amazing movie. It was the training sequences that made it fascinating and involving. It also secured Liu Chia Hui a star.

Director Liu's oeuvre is explored until its end, focusing for a time on *Legendary Weapons of China* (U.S. title, *Legendary Weapons of Kung Fu*), of which the authors write:

> [It is] the quintessential martial arts movie. It is Liu Chi Liang's best movie and possibly the best genre film ever.

The authors have their reasons for that assessment, and they reveal it in their discussion of the film. But the one thing that director Liu added that was new was magic. Kung fu magic. Kung fu magician/spies are the source of the Ninjas, the authors write. More to the point, the magic in this film was the seed that sprouted whole forests of kung fu movies in which people fly and wheel and spin strange energies between their hands that they can then shoot out to wound their enemies or strike them dead.

The next chapter covers Jackie Chan, from his childhood to superstardom. Now, forty years later, Chan remains a martial arts movie favorite for his skill, humor, and self-deprecation, not to mention for doing his own stunts. Writing about Chan naturally brings in Sammo Hung and Yuen Baio. Other more contemporary martial arts stars, such as Jet Li, are mentioned, but this was too early in his career for the authors to have much to write about him. And of course, Donnie Yen wasn't even on the horizon.

This ends the section on Chinese kung fu cinema, and now the authors turn their attention to Japanese martial arts movies. These mostly are samurai films of one sort or another, with swordplay being the draw, rather than open-hand combat. As with the section on China's martial arts cinema, this section begins with a brief history of Japan and its martial arts culture. This amply sets the stage for understanding the core characteristics of what might otherwise be termed Samurai Cinema.

After the history, the authors describe a number of Japanese martial arts styles, although they include in the mix Hapkido, Taekwondo, and oddly, Savate. Although they rightly call Hapkido and Taekwondo Korean arts, they stumble in calling Savate a French variation on karate. Nothing could be farther from the truth. Savate was developed in northern France, particularly in the slums of Paris, and later, in fact, influenced karate by introducing high kicks, such as the roundhouse.

The authors then move on to discuss the early sword slashers of Japanese cinema, called chambara movies. These, the authors state, feature as many sword styles as Chinese martial arts movies do kung fu styles. Several early stars of this genre are touched on, but the true hero wasn't a swordsman or star, but a director: Akira Kurosawa. Almost singlehandedly, Kurosawa introduced true art into his films to bolster the action with meaningful human interaction, conflict, and resolution. And Kurosawa discovered and introduced one of chambara films' first potent hero/anti-hero actors in the person of Toshiro Mifune.

The films that both men worked on together are dissected, then the text segues easily into a look at the Zatoichi film series, starring Shintaro Katsu. Zatoichi is a blind master swordsman who doesn't look at all like a warrior, traveling around medieval Japan and coming to the aid of the downtrodden, all while on the run from gangsters, bounty hunters, and challengers.

The films of Raizo Ichikawa are featured next, these about the character of Kyoshiro Nemuri, dubbed "Son of Black Mass" due to the evil circumstances of his birth. Nemuri is an amoral adventurer who, in the Son of Black Mass film series, travels around, cutting people up, raping women, and generally behaving like a degenerate. However, the authors state:

> Would you believe the these movies were done with high style and surprising taste? It's true. Although beyond the comprehension of many Western eyes, the Nemuri movies were done with demure sophistication.

They go on to write:

> The Son of Black Mass movies stand on their own, without these defenses. At their heart, they promoted a belief in oneself. They also soundly condemned the society that allowed such a tortured halfbreed as Kyoshiro Nemuri to exist.

One of the Son of Black Mass series' most lasting influences was its introduction of Ninjas to the cinematic martial arts mix, adding a whole category of bad guys for the martial arts hero to confront and wipe out.

The next subject the authors examine is the Baby Cart to Hell film series, starring Shintaro Katsu's real-life brother, Tomisaburo Wakayama. The Son of Black Mass films might have been demure and practically bloodless, but the Baby Cart to Hell films were anything but, splashing blood everywhere and occasionally featuring nudity. There is even one scene in which the hero is forced at sword point to rape a woman, for which he apologizes to her beforehand. Afterhand, he slaughters those who forced the act.

This is where Japanese martial arts films take a departure from the chambara to open-hand karate combat thanks to the films of Sonny Chiba. The authors recognize the groundswell that traded the swords and medieval settings for fists and modern settings, and they also recognize the growing brutality of the genre expressed in Chiba's expressly violent and gory films. The really bad thing, they say, is that Chiba's films just aren't very good in terms of character, plot, or even storytelling. Here's how they characterize matters at the end of the chapter:

> The Chinese and Japanese cinema started at opposite poles and moved in opposite directions. The Chinese started with junk and worked toward excellence. The Japanese stated at excellence and are moving toward junk.

Chapter five takes the martial arts cinema story to America. It begins with actor/writer/director/martial artist Tom Laughlin's *Billy Jack* and its cinematic offsprings. Laughlin's background leads into the introduction of the Billy Jack character in *Born Losers* and its development through the succeeding three films. The authors aren't always kind to Laughlin, but they concede that he helped elevate martial arts movies in America by adding a layer of social/ethical conflict as a trigger for martial action justice, rather than the trigger simply being revenge.

Then, just as American martial arts movie-goers had to, the authors struggle through a series of films and filmmakers, such as the team of producer Jerry Weintraub and director Robert Clouse who valiantly tried to replicate the success of their *Enter the Dragon* and repeatedly failed.

There were dozens of these sorts of dead ends in American martial arts cinema of the time, and the authors go into several of them—*The Challenge, Firecracker, Kill or Be Killed,* and *Kill the Golden Goose,* and others. There was even, *A Fistful of Yen,* an extended parody of *Enter the Dragon* featured in *Kentucky Fried Movie.* The problem at the time was that most actors couldn't convincingly do martial arts and most martial artists couldn't act.

Chuck Norris couldn't act, but he could do martial arts, and he is featured next. The authors conclude that, while his martial arts films did well enough, particularly in the beginning, his lack of thespian chops and screen presence eventually doomed his career and kept him from superstardom.

Ninjas come next.

Ninjas.

Ninjas and Sho Kosugi.

And that's the end except for several lists. One names the ten best martial arts movies of all time, another names the twenty-five best kung fu videos, and a third names the twenty-five worse kung fu videos. These lists, being from 1985, certainly can't now claim to be "of all time," but they do reflect the state of martial arts cinema up to that point. The book ends with a list of martial arts actors using their screen names and then giving their actual names and other pseudonyms. This is a nice addition, as are the cutlines for the photos, which identify the people in the shots. Unfortunately, the book completely lacks an index.

Structurally, probably less than half the book is text, the remainder being photos. Most often these are stills, but there also are lots of movie posters. Everything is in black and white, even the posters. The text is well written, but for my taste, this book, while better than Verina Glaessner's *Kung Fu: Cinema of Vengeance,* still relies too much on retelling plot lines and too little on analysis. However, the authors do often touch on the interplay between the martial arts—and its cinema—and China and Japan's cultural history as well as the (early) effects that martial arts cinema had on American culture. In the end, this book is a pleasant and informative journey through a well-loved genre.

And it's fun to look at the photos of all those movies I watched on television back in the 1980s.

The Kung Fu Book of Caine
The Complete Guide to TV's First Mystical Eastern Western

By Herbie J. Pilato
(Charles E. Tuttle Co., 1993, 206 pages)

Even with the astronomical proliferation of martial arts films and television programs during the past fifty years, it is entirely possible that no single example is as well-known worldwide as *Kung Fu*, starring David Carradine. The original series aired a movie-length pilot and sixty-two fifty-minute episodes over three seasons from October 1972 to April 1975. The show not only introduced Chinese kung fu to the general Western audience, it also brought with it a healthy dose of Taoist and Buddhist wisdom, also unfamiliar to Westerners. Most people regard *Kung Fu* as a martial arts program, but really it is a family drama. Kwai Chang comes to America to search for family, and all of the sequels feature his literal offspring and those who came after them. Even today there is an addition, and even if its woman hero bears no familial relationship to Kwai Chang, she is one of his spiritual successors. In addition, many, if not most, of the episodes involve families of one sort or another in need of succor or healing.

To my knowledge, *The Kung Fu Book of Caine* was the first book devoted to the show, and though there might be others, I am not aware of them. But this one is enough, covering almost every aspect of the show's inception, development, production, and aftermath that it could at the time of its publication.

The book opens, appropriately enough, with a foreword by Kwai Chang Caine himself: David Carradine. He writes:

> Way back in the prehistoric seventies…a bunch of us started shooting a movie for TV called Kung Fu. We had no idea what it would lead to; we just thought it was a really great script.

The foreword was written while *Kung Fu, The Legend Continues* was in production, and it's a straightforward, well-written piece on how the original series exploded, how he dealt with that, and how he developed the character of Kwai Chang. Along the way, he reveals a few interesting factoids regarding the several motifs that ran continuously through the series. The primary one was fidelity to the Taoist and Buddhist precepts that molded Kwai Chang's personality, but the others are less philosophical.

For example, at the beginning of the series, Carradine started with a shaved head, and from then on, he did not cut his hair at all until the final episode, when he shaved it again. Thus, he says, you can roughly gauge an episode's placement in the series by the length of his hair. Another example is that, upon hearing of Bruce Lee's death, he changed the color of his shirt from brown to saffron to mark that sad event. He also talks about the flutes. The many flutes. In fact, Carradine continued to make and play flutes throughout the rest of the life.

After a short preface by the author, the book opens with "Part One: The Making of Kung Fu." This section lays out the show's premise and the nature of Kwai Chang Caine's character. Carradine is quoted as saying:

> One thing I figured out for myself was that the story was not about truth, it was about love.

But it also was about love in conflict with all the negative qualities of human character: greed, violence, hatred, intolerance, arrogance, indifference…the list seems never-ending. And those conflicts gave viewers at least one, and usually two, fight scenes in which Caine was compelled to use his skills. I've written elsewhere about Carradine's personal kung fu skills, which were obviously nil in the pilot but which visibly improved during the course of the series.

Many elements, of course, contributed to the show's success, and Pilato covers them ably. Throughout are quotes by the people, aside from Carradine, who made the show possible: the writers, directors, producers, and other actors, giving real personality to the show's development. The story begins with Ed Spielman, who, as a teenager, was enchanted with Japanese samurai movies. He studied martial arts while he was in college, and it was then that he first learned about kung fu. Years later, while attempting to write a comedy script with his friend, Howard Friedlander, the two found the idea morphing into an idea for a kung fu movie. The original setting was to be China, with an American partnering up with a Shaolin monk, but Friedlander suggested they flip it around and make an Eastern Western, with the monk coming to the American Wild West.

They wrote the script, which came to the attention of Jerry Thorpe, who was looking for a unique project to produce and direct and found it in Spielman and Friedlander's script. The final element was to give the character of Kwai Chang a reason for his wanderings, and so his journey became a search for family, which was symbolic of his search for self-identity. The role Bruce Lee played in the project as it developed is given some space.

A chapter on the styles, practices, and tenets of Shaolin kung fu leads to one on the character of Kwai Chang. His unfamiliarity with his new American surroundings allows the writers to define those surroundings in nontraditional, often critical ways to point out social, political, and cultural ills. This sets up natural situational conflicts that are apt fodder for morality plays on an incredible variety of topics, such as slavery, greed, cruelty, intolerance, corruption, and even mental illness, among many others.

The use of different actors to portray Kwai Chang at earlier stages of his life is discussed, as is the development of the character over the course of his "life." Carradine, in particular, has a number of things to say about how he approached the character. The author also delves into the choice of Carradine, a non-Asian, to play an Asian character and how the Asian-American acting community reacted. In general, the Association of Asian/Pacific American Artists felt that Carradine was an artistically good fit for the role, and even more, the group appreciated the boost the show gave to the careers of the numerous Asian-American who populated the cast of masters and other supporting characters. Some of these folks are the subject of the next chapter. Pilato does not go into the accusations of yellow-face and other racial and gender biases that have dogged the show since it aired.

A chapter on technical matters follows. The first element it looks at is the sets for the Shaolin temple, which were originally constructed for the 1967 film, *Camelot*, and redone for the 1973 remake of *Lost Horizon* before being dressed up once more, this time in Shaolin clothing for *Kung Fu*. Even film sets have to play different roles and assume different costumes. Located in Burbank, the set was the largest in America at the time. Pilato writes about the show's props next, including Caine's flutes, then he moves on to a discussion of the series' film techniques and visual effects. Some of these, such as specific camera techniques, were groundbreaking and added significantly to the visual language of film and video.

Makeup effects comes next, and this was an important element given the number of younger actors who had to appear to be old and how many bald heads showed up in each episode. Radamas Pera, who played the young Caine, describes the dilemma of either being the only bald kid in school or opting for hours of sitting in painstaking makeup sessions. Preferring a head of hair, he did the latter, and though he hated the sessions, he had a liking for makeup artist Frank Westmore, of the famed Westmore family of movie makeup artists. Actor James Hong, whose long and prolific career spans numerous genres, also speaks highly of Westmore. The contact lenses that Key Luke wore to make him look blind as Master Po also get a little space.

Then, over the next hundred pages, the author catalogs the series, beginning with the pilot and working his way through to the end. Each entry lists the episode number and title, followed by the names of the writers, director, and principal guest actors. After that is a two- or three-paragraph synopsis and a paragraph of interesting factoids about the episode or its cast. Black-and-white stills from the show are randomly scattered throughout.

The next chapter, titled, "The Return of Caine," takes a look Caine's reappearances during the two decades between the end of the show in 1975 and the publication of this book. They begin with a cameo in the Kenny Rogers vehicle, *Gambler Four: Luck of the Draw* and an appearance in a parody on *Saturday Night Live*. Carradine says that those were tests to see if he could still play the character.

Apparently he was convinced, because he initiated the production of *Kung Fu: The Movie* (1986), featuring a realistically older Kwai Chang. This was followed the next year by the little-remembered, *Kung Fu: The Next Generation*, with David Darlow as Kwai Chang's grandson, also named Kwai Chang Caine, and Brandon Lee as his budding delinquent son, Johnny Caine. This TV pilot, though largely forgotten now, was a decent attempt to launch the *Kung Fu* series into a contemporary urban setting.

Pilato devotes an entire chapter to *Kung Fu: The Legend Continues*, in which Carradine once again takes the helm as…wait for it: The original Kwai Chang Caine's grandson—though not, of course, the same grandson as in *The Next Generation*. And he can't even be a brother grandson since Carradine's new Caine is also named Kwai Chang. Like his alter ego, who must exist in another timeline, he also has a son, though this one's name is Peter. A police detective, Peter is different in every way from Johnny Caine except in their hot-headed recklessness. The setting, though, is still contemporary urban. Also in an urban setting is the 2021 adaptation, *Kung Fu*, starring Olivia Liang, which has been renewed for two more seasons. So, apparently, the *Kung Fu* legend does continue.

The last section of the book is a series of appendices, beginning with selected bios of principal cast members and production people. These are short and usually to the point, but one element lacking is the martial arts background of David Chow, the original kung fu advisor for the series. Chow does say in the section devoted to his involvement that he was simply in the right place at the right time. In other words, he knew some kung fu and he also knew somebody who was looking for someone who knew some kung fu. But he gives no clues to his training and who he learned from, although his bio reveals an interesting fellow whose life outside of Kung Fu was quite remarkable.

The next appendix is a list of Emmy nominations and awards, followed by one showing a sample shooting schedule for the show—specifically December 11, 1973. The book ends with a good index.

Fight scenes on TV and in film have improved exponentially over the years since *Kung Fu* first hit the screen, and it's easy to look at the ones on *Kung Fu* with a jaundiced eye. But then, consider the alternatives available at the time: Japanese samurai films, fewer than a handful of Bruce Lee films, and dozens upon dozens of turgid Hong Kong chopsocky films, most of which had not yet appeared on American TV. With those as a backdrop, *Kung Fu* presented an open atmosphere and dramatic—and often spiritual—learning experiences because, obviously, the fight, while sometimes necessary, isn't the important thing. The people are. If you're not fighting for someone or some humane principal, you're just fostering brutality. That is the real lesson of Kwai Chang Caine's journey to the West and why that lesson will remain long after the dust of combat has settled.

The Kung Fu Book of Caine is recommended for those interested in the general history of the martial arts in media representations and in the development of this series in particular.

Part VII

Booklets and Pamphlets

Introduction

In this section, I'm going to tackle something you don't see much of these days: booklets and pamphlets. Publications such as these, along with newsletters and some other sorts of printed matter, have largely fallen by the wayside, supplanted by webpages on the Internet, print-on-demand publishing, and e-books. But back in the days before personal computers, people who had something to say that wasn't long enough for a book or that couldn't otherwise find a mainstream publication venue would put together a small publication, sometimes with typesetting done on a typewriter, basic graphics, and quick-copy or photocopy reproduction.

Occasionally, these sorts of booklets and pamphlets were produced and distributed by publication companies, and a few of them might even have ended up in bookstores. But just as often, they were amateur to semi-professional products intended for small circulation among members of a group, school, organization, or club. These sorts of publications tend to be of varying quality, not only in production values but in the information they contain. Sometimes, they hold some degree of complexity or substance, and at others, they're little more than curiosity pieces.

Most of these booklets were not available to the general public at the time of their publication, and a great many of them probably enjoyed only a limited number of copies. Such publications are part of what used to be known as the small press movement, which died upon the advent of the Internet. Small press publishers were anything from amateur one-timers to long-term hobbyists to serious avocational practitioners, and their publications occupied the void between a writer's own filing cabinets and professional regional and mainstream publications. They were the training ground—and the dumping ground—for a wide variety of efforts, usually centered around specific topics. Popular types were poetry and literary magazines and sci-fi fanzines. You could rightly call the material I'll look at in this section as martial arts small press, even if some of it brushed the edges of "legitimate" publication.

To be clear, I'm distinguishing booklet- and pamphlet-style publications from periodical-style publications, such as magazines, journals, newsletters, and digests. Booklets and pamphlets are usually one-off efforts, while periodicals are on-going for a shorter or longer span of time in the form of serial issues. Also, I'm not talking about brochures, flyers, and hand-out types of literature, all of which, though one-offs, are of a lesser scope.

Undoubtedly, there are hundreds—perhaps thousands—of these martial arts small press publications floating around out there, though my collection of martial arts literature contains only those reviewed below. Be aware that many of these are no longer available except by accident or good fortune—which, according to the Taoist sage, are the same thing. Hey, maybe there's a secret yet ultimate Taiji manual out there in some salt shop or bookstall, just waiting to be chanced upon!

Finally, a note on typesetting: These days, anyone can produce professional quality typesetting at home, but in the days before personal computers, professional typesetting had to be done on specialized typesetting equipment, and that cost bucks. Some of the publishers of small press publications opted for that, but others went the home-production route by setting body type on a typewriter and headlines with an obsolete graphics technology called rub-on type. An average typewriter with a cloth ribbon produces inferior-quality type for the purposes of reproduction. The letters will be both blobby and broken. Higher-quality typewriters, such as the IBM Selectric, which use carbon ribbons and have interchangeable fonts, produced sharper, higher-quality results, though still not quite those of professional typesetting.

Tai Chi Chuan

by Her Yue Wong
(Her Yue Wong, 1973, 60 pages)

First, we'll look at *Tai Chi Chuan* by Her Yue Wong. Published in 1973 by the author, this booklet is a perfect example of the most basic of these sorts of publications. A note on the back cover indicates that Wong was in Oklahoma City at the time of publication, but as far as I can recollect, he moved to Houston, Texas, and taught Taiji there in a park. I met him very briefly at the Southwest United States Kung Fu / Wushu Exposition, held in Houston in 1986. I heard this story about how he started teaching: His first students were his kids, who wanted to learn Taiji from him, He said fine, he'd teach them as long as they kept up their grades and went to college. They did, and he taught them. I don't know if the story is apocryphal or not, but it's a good one.

His publication is a saddle-stitched, 5.5"x8.5" booklet with poor-quality type set on a regular typewriter. Usually, a booklet of this type was reproduced and trimmed in a small printing operation rather than by photocopy—especially when this booklet was published since photocopy operations at the time were still pretty crude.

Wong starts out with a short preface that leads into the standard Chang Sanfeng legend, with the caveat that no one is really certain about the origins of Taiji. He mentions three major styles of Taiji and the names of a few masters, all without context. The next section outlines the principles of kung fu in general and Taiji specifically, the idea of chi, and how Taiji integrates yin and yang. It's all very cursory but completely straightforward and genuine. Next is a form list for a long Yang style form, and the rest of the booklet—fifty-two pages—is form instruction, with adequate text and well-done line drawings that include arrows to indicate the direction of limb and body movements.

Obviously, Wong's students were the intended audience for this booklet, and it probably suited it's intended purpose well. If Wong had expanded the expository material, the book could have found wider publication since these sorts of books were burgeoning at the time. My copy was autographed on the cover by Wong in 1979, but he did that for someone else, not me, and I don't remember how or where I acquired this copy.

William Chen's Tai Chi Chuan

by William C. C. Chen
(The William C. C. Chen School of T'ai-chi Ch'uan, 1973, 62 pages)

Next on our list of small-press martial arts publications is *William C. C. Chen's Tai Chi Chuan*. This publication falls in the middle of the spectrum of our subject. It is actually more of a little book than a booklet, being 4.25"x7" and perfect-bound. It is sixty-two pages long, with a mixture of typesetting. The introductory material appears to be professionally typeset, while the captions for the photos in the instruction section appear to be set on a good quality typewriter. The instruction section features excellently reproduced, if small, photos of Chen performing the form. After all, this is a small book.

The brief introductory material begins with a one-page foreword. Even if it doesn't really say much, it is by none other than Robert W. Smith. This is followed by an introduction that's obviously not written by Chen since it refers to "Master Chen" in the third person, but no matter. It is only four pages—small pages, remember—but not bad, considering its brevity. After a thumbnail tale of Chang Sanfeng being inspired to create Taiji while watching a fight between a snake and bird, the writer gives thumbnail definitions of several principles that underlie Taiji, all of which are valid and excellent, such as relaxation, slowness, diaphragmatic breathing, single-weightedness, circularity, and unity of movement. There's not a lot of discussion here, but these are very important points to keep in mind and body when performing Taiji, and here they're succinctly and clearly stated.

The next page gives some context to the time frame during which most of the booklets and pamphlets I'm discussing in this series were published. This context is a small notice stating:

> For those interested in seeing the complete flow of T'ai Chi Ch'uan movements, there is a "super 8" film available for sale.

The contact information follows. This page is interesting for a couple of reasons. First and foremost, of course, is that the home-viewing medium is super-8 film. Since then, Chen has been seen on a succession of different visual formats: videotape, DVD, and *YouTube*. And that points to the other interesting aspect: It shows that Chen is not only a master of Taiji but a masterful innovator in the dissemination of the art via a medium that can graphically display the entire flow of the movements.

Returning to Chen's little book: Almost the entire remainder is filled with photos of Chen performing a sixty-movement Taiji sequence. Each major movement is depicted in two to six photos, with arrows. The names of the movements are at the tops of the pages, but there is no explanatory text. Chen is fairly young here, and his posture is a little more erect than I've seen in some later film footage of him doing his form, in which he was extremely sung. Two pages of similar photos of two young women pushing hands, with arrows, close out the book.

Although the production values are a little better than those of Wong's booklet, Chen's little book has the same intended audience—his students—and wasn't produced for sale in a bookshop. I don't remember how or where I got this one, either.

Quick and Easy T'ai-chi Ch'uan
Eight Simple Chinese Exercises for Health

by Yang Ming-shih
(Shufunotomo Co, Ltd., 1974, 61 pages)

The next booklet represents the most professional of these types of publications, and was published by a company that apparently produced other entries on Chinese and Japanese subjects, such as cooking, flower arrangement, and bonsai, in what the company called the "Quick &  Easy Series." These are 6"x4.25" booklets with comb binding. *Quick & Easy T'ai-chi Ch'uan* is by Yang Ming-shih—yes, of those Yangs.

Q&ETC is sixty-two pages long, and very thick pages they are: every page is heavy card stock that is coated on one side. Coated means that the paper stock has a glossy or semi-glossy coating applied to one or both sides. The reason for the coating is that photographs reproduce more crisply on coated stock than on uncoated stock, which will soak up a little of the ink, blurring the image slightly. Ink can't soak into coated stock, so there's no blurring. With all those thick pages and comb binding, this booklet reminds me of some of the children's books I bought my daughters when they were young—the kinds of books that are hard for toddlers to destroy and whose pages are easy for their little, inexperienced fingers to turn.

I guess the idea of the books in the Q&E series is that you can use them to learn to do something relatively simple, and that the comb binding allows the books to lie flat on a table so you can refer to them while your hands are otherwise occupied with the activity depicted in the book. (See the sample open page to the right.) The secret to the fact that the activity in this Taiji booklet is not actually Taiji lies in the subtitle: *Eight Simple Chinese Exercises for Health.*

The exercises are chi kung that concentrate on movement rather than breathing, all done in a moderate horse stance of slightly varying height. They form, in fact, a venerable chi kung sequence known as the Eight Brocades, although the book does not name them as such. The Eight Brocades is a chi kung sequence that has been around for centuries, and while it does have an energy component, it is only moderate, with many of the movements focusing more on developing the tendon system and opening the body rather than on directly strengthening the meridian system and chi flow.

Each exercise occupies several flip pages, and the photos are accompanied by basic instructions. The exercises are all pretty good, and while they aren't Taiji, they are strung together into a sequential routine that is a simple-to-learn but effective daily practice of light intensity and moderate duration.

Personally, I'll stick with the several chi kung I already do, which also open the body but that are more energy-oriented than the Eight Brocades, and I'll let my Taiji deal with tendon development. But the Eight Brocades might work for you, particularly if you don't want to practice Taiji. It's possible that this book could be found via the Internet. It had a cover price then of $2.50 and was distributed by Japan Publications, which published other titles of interest to martial artists, such as *Acupuncture Medicine* by Yoshiaki Omura. (Reviewed earlier in this volume.) But even if you can't find it, instructions for the Eight Brocades can be found in many places, such as the Internet and martial arts/chi kung books and magazines.

Pa-Kua
The Gentle Art of Health

by John Painter
(Paper Lantern Publishing Company, 1986, 18 pages)

The intro to this slight booklet reads, "This complimentary copy of the *Pa Kua Chang Healing Arts* by Dr. John P. Painter, based upon the Spring Rain Ch'i Kung exercises of Professor Li Ch'ing Yuen's Nine Dragon Pa Kua Chang art, is distributed by *Internal Arts Magazine* to Charter subscribers only. The material in this manual is excerpted from Dr. Painter's book *Pa Kua Chang Taoist Boxing for Health & Self-defense*. [Paper Lantern Publishing Company]."

The booklet, then, is essentially a marketing tool for Painter's book, but even so, it contains some interesting information on Bagua. It starts off with a brief introduction to the history and art of Bagua, but it quickly moves on to its main subject: Bagua's effects on health and well-being. It cites data gathered on Bagua by an organization called the Life Sciences Institute, though that organization is now a little hard to pin down. There is a collaborative, independent research institution called the Life Sciences Institute at the University of Michigan in Ann Arbor, but it was founded in 1999, so it probably isn't the same organization as the one named by Painter.[1] There also is an International Life Sciences Institute in Washington, D.C., founded in 1978, but this organization's members are primarily food and beverage, agricultural, chemical, and pharmaceutical companies, so it probably isn't the one Painter was talking about, either.[2] And then there's the California Life Sciences Institute.... Well, you see where this is going. Painter's pamphlet was produced more than thirty years ago. Who knows which Life Sciences Institute he's referring to, or even if the right one is still in operation.

Nonetheless, Painter presents data from this institute in a chapter titled, "A Report on the Effects of Pa Kua Chang and Its Effects on Physical Conditioning and Health," which data, he confesses, was still being acquired at the time of the writing. A cursory Internet search did not turn up a copy of this report. According to Painter, the researchers gathered data on aerobic capacity, strength development, flexibility, production of relaxation response, and overall health improvement fostered by Bagua. He doesn't give complete data on all of these aspects, but he gives samples of studies of heart rate, which show a reduction in cardiovascular rates following a round of Bagua. In addition, the data showed a marked decrease in intercellular body fat as well as an increase in flexibility. Studies of stress management also showed greater relaxation following the set.

"Beneficial Effects of Pa Kua Chang" is the title of the next section, and it contains mostly anecdotal references to the Bagua master Li Ch'ing Yuen, followed by a list of Bagua's benefits to the body, mind, and spirit. I won't enumerate those here, but they're pretty much what you'd expect—both with respect to Master Li's skills and Bagua's benefits—and this material could just as easily be a bio of a Taiji master and a list of Taiji benefits.

Next, the text discusses how "the methods of Pa Kua Chang and her two sister arts—Taijiquan and Xingyi Chuan—offer an unrealized source of rehabilitative energy to those in need of healing and rejuvenation." After this, Painter goes into Bagua's effects on the lymphatic system, which increases the art's positive impact on the practitioner's health and well-being.

Painter then presents the introductory material for the Spring Rain Cleansing Exercises, a series of eight chi kung exercises performed while walking around the Bagua circle. But before he actually demonstrates the eight exercises, he pauses to discuss diaphragmatic breathing, the basic methods of walking the Bagua circle, how to step and turn properly to avoid injuring the knees, and the eight roundings of Bagua—namely holding major joints in rounded rather than angular postures. The eight exercises themselves are run through in two pages. The book's final page seems to be a continuation of the general instructions on walking the circle, with a discussion of stance height added.

Pa-Kua: The Gentle Art of Health has a simple saddle-stitched construction, and the type was set with a typewriter, but the cover is printed on coated stock. It is a unique pamphlet of its type since it does not go into form—except for the Spring Rain Chi Kung form—but mostly discusses other aspects of Bagua in a more expository fashion.

Notes
1 "Life Sciences Institute," *Wikipedia*, https://en.wikipedia.org/wiki/Life_Sciences_Institute
2 "International Life Sciences Institute," *Wikipedia*, https://en.wikipedia.org/wiki/International_Life_Sciences_Institute
3 California Life Sciences Institute website: http://califesciencesinstitute.org/

Dragonbolt
A Bora-Yong (Purple Dragon) Self-defense Course

by D. H. Elder, Jr.
(Bora-Yong Martial Arts Club, 1975, 24 pages)

Dragonbolt, Priest's Lightning Bolt (PLB), Yarawa, and Kubotan are all names for a short stick held in the hand that can be used in fighting, and that weapon is the subject of this booklet. Elder opens the text with a several-page tale of a young priest using a PLB to subdue a gang of bandits who accosted him during a journey to another temple. It's a fun if familiar story, and it demonstrates the cloaked nature as well as the effectiveness of this weapon when wielded in skillful hands.

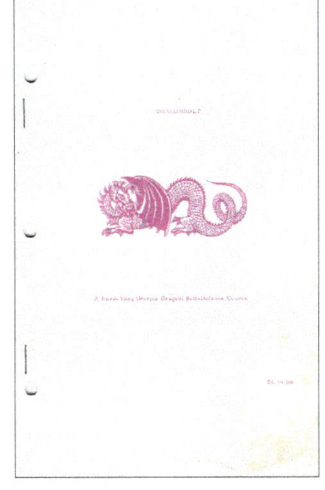

The next chapter looks at different configurations of the PLB, both in materials and profiles. What it leaves out is the idea that a great number of items can substitute for a store-bought PLB, such as pens, lipstick tubes, short bones, or nearly anything that's about 6" long and of sufficient diameter that you can grip it without it slipping out of your hand and that isn't so flimsy that it will bend or shatter when you strike a target with its end. Heck, you can even use the stiff corner of a wallet, cellphone, or other object that can be held in the hand.

The next section on grip and stances emphasizes the user's ability to conceal the PLB in the palm, gripping it only when using it to strike at vulnerable targets, such as pressure points and cavities. These are illustrated, front and back, and ways to strike them singly or in combination also are given. This is pretty solid if sketchy material, marred by the author's obvious anti-liberal stance. Sorry, Mr. Elder, but most liberals I know would kick an assailant's ass, too. The only difference between them and you is that they'd probably feel bad about it afterwards, while you, apparently, would gloat.

Then, after warning would-be martial artists to study only with qualified instructors, the booklet presents an ad for the the Bora-Yong Martial Arts Club, which you could join for only $5. Your membership included a discount on items purchased from the club. Items advertised on the next few pages include Dragonbolts in various configurations, nunchuka, and three-section staffs. Closing out the book is a page advertising Bora-Yong Martial Arts Club's six other booklets—with "more to come" printed at the bottom of the page. Whether or not further booklets did appear is unknown to me, as are the contents of the other six booklets the club did publish.

Dragonbolt has typewriter type that is double-spaced, so the information it contains is about half of what the pages could have held. The handful of illustrations are crisp. The cover is printed on a light-weight coated stock, but oddly, there is no pretense at binding—the pages are simply stapled together.

Tai Chi Sabre for Self-defense

edited by Tom Marks
translated by Dominic Liu
(McLisa Enterprises, 1975, 52 pages)

Next we'll look at *Tai Chi Sabre for Self-defense*, edited by Tom Marks and translated by Dominic Liu. This is a curious little piece, published in 1975, that raises a couple of questions. Like William C. C. Chen's publication covered above, *Tai Chi Sabre* is a little book. It is 5"x7.5", uses professional typesetting throughout, and is perfect-bound in a faux reptile-skin cover stock that has brittled and discolored with age. And there's something else that's a little brittle and discolored: the content.

Tom Marks is listed as "Captain Tom Marks" on the title page, and his bio says he was born in 1950 and graduated from West Point in 1972. That was followed by a three-year tour in Hawaii, where he earned an MA in Asian history at the University of Hawaii. He also "travelled extensively in Asia, having spent some five months in the Republic of China." This takes him up to to 1975—the same year in which this book was published. When Marks was 25 years old.

There is no mention in the bio of his martial arts training, though he did compete and coach in track-and-field, and he published articles on Asia in academic and professional journals. However, he could have learned Taiji in Hawaii. Early Western Taiji adopter Edward Maisel, author of *Tai Chi for Health* (reviewed in

Volume VI of this series), learned Taiji in Hawaii a decade or more before Marks went there to study Asian history at the University of Hawaii. It's possible that Marks could have gained an interest in Taiji given his college major, but when we consider that he was young and had spent most of his life in America, it's reasonable to assume that if he had any training at all, it was only of three or so years' duration. That is, if he actually had any real training and that this book isn't simply an exercise in academic publication.

The first clues that there is something fishy about this book come after Marks's one-page preface, in a chapter titled "The Tai Chi Sabre Method." This chapter lays out ten important points or principles to follow while practicing with the saber. The ten points are sound and valid, but the problem arises because they are, point for point, exactly the same ten principles detailed in a chapter in *Tai Chi Tao* by Cai Long titled "The Knacks in the Exercise of Tai Chi Tao." (See reviews for two translations of this book in Volume IV of this series.) The language in each is slightly different, but the content of the statements and the order in which the information appears show that both are from a single original source. Comparing the two, Long's is more explicit and thorough, making the Marks version seem like a paraphrase.

The Marks book then presents a translated poem titled "Formulas of the Tai Chi Sabre," which could just as easily been titled, "Song of the Tai Chi Saber." This poem does not appear in the Long book, but after that, almost all dissimilarities vanish. Both books go on to present illustrations that, though different in style, depict exactly the same saber form using exactly the same postures, at exactly the same angles, with exactly the same arrows to show direction of movement, in exactly the same number of movements, with extremely similar text to describe each movement. This text is somewhat more thorough in the Long book. The only real difference is that the Marks book has line-drawings while the Long book has photos of a man named Sin Man Ho, who is not credited in the book. But I know it's him because he served a similar duty in posing for the photos in Li Zhen's, *Illustrations of Thirteen Tai-chi Sword*, where he was identified. (Reviewed in Volume IV of this series)

Because of these many similarities, it's important to note the almost minuscule differences. The line drawings in the Marks book are not tracings of the photos of Sin Man Ho, and while the drawings and photos bear a striking similarity throughout in angle and sameness of posture, there are a couple of minor differences—in one posture, for example, in the exact angle of a lower leg dangling from an upraised knee. But in each case, Sin's posture is more capable looking than the one in Marks's similar line drawing, just as Long's text is more thorough than Marks's.

Both books end after the instruction section, leaving us with two possible scenarios regarding authorship, which we know is not by Marks:

1.) Long is the original author, the translator of this English version is unknown (just as the performer is uncredited), and the Marks version is an unauthorized and unattributed translation that appeared at an earlier date.

2.) Long is not the original author but was, like Marks, only a translator of another original source that also was translated by Marks. Either or both versions might be unauthorized and unattributed.

There is one bit of information that argues for the first assumption: the existence of the other translation of this book, published in 1959 and titled, *Taiji Saber*, with the author listed as Cai Longyue. This one uses a different set of photos/illustrations than either of the other two books. (See review in Volume IV of this series.)

The only words in English on the cover of the book attributed to Cai Long are the title and a notice printed on the back: "Published and Printed in Hong Kong." No author on the cover. The title page holds only the title, the author's name, and the notice: "Chinese-English," which refers to the fact that the text contains Chinese characters as well as the English translation. The copyright page has the publisher and distributor information, but nowhere is there any information about the book itself, such as the original source. Nor is there a bio of Long or any other background on the book or the form it depicts.

It might be said that any two—or three—books that depict and describe exactly the same form might look equally similar and read much the same. Yes, they might, but not so exactly the same in terms of illustration or so nearly the same in text. I've seen plenty of such descriptions of various forms in books on Taiji and other martial arts, and none are as alike as these two, even if the Marks version is slightly inferior. Because that inferiority might indicate a lack of true familiarity with the saber, I find it to be suspicious.

Further—and aside from Marks's youth and lack of documented experience as a martial artist—his source is unattributed, though one Dominic Liu is named as translator. So, perhaps as "editor," Marks just pulled the book together from a translation of an unsourced Chinese book and illustrations of an equally unknown origin, to which he added a brief foreword and his name as author. Or maybe he just appropriated Cai's book and called it his own.

Defenders of Marks might point out that his book came out first, but the fact that Long's book in English was not published until 1980 is meaningless in terms of which book is more original, particularly since Long's book originally appeared in 1959. At bottom, I have serious doubts about Marks' version and its provenance, and it seems to me a case of blatant plagiarism.

Tom Marks's *Tai Chi Sabre*, apparently, did not enjoy a reprint, but used copies can be found online for $30 and up. It might be worth it as a collector's item, but I also must say that I taught myself Cai Long's sabere form from his book, and this one's almost exactly the same, so it would be possible to learn the form from this one, too. Just remember that its cover is as brittle as its provenance.

Chen Taijiquan
The Inner Circle of Secrecy

by Michael A. DeMarco
(Michael A. DeMarco, 1986, 24 pages)

The next publication we'll consider is *Chen Taijiquan: The Inner Circle of Secrecy*, by Michael A. DeMarco. This booklet was published in 1986, and in production values it is almost identical to Her Yue Wong's book, discussed above: a 5.5"x8.5", saddle-stitched booklet that uses typewriter typesetting. Unlike Wong's booklet, however, which was a basic instruction manual for Wong's students, DeMarco's booklet is, in fact, an early academic-style publication on Taiji. But unlike *Tai Chi Sabre* by Tom Marks, this one doesn't piggy-back off the work of others—at least not in a plagiaristic way.

Instead, this is a monograph on Taiji history, focusing on Chen Style. It's worth noting at the outset that this monograph was written at a time when American understanding of Taiji history was sketchy and when awareness of Chen Style was in its infancy.

In the introduction, DeMarco lays out his purposes: 1) to firmly establish Chen Village as the place of origin of Taijiquan; 2) to show the evolution of Taiji in terms of the personal manners and martial attributes of the masters of Chen and other styles; 3) to examine the social aspects of Taiji and how and why the art was, for many centuries, protected by clan members; 4) and finally, to show that Chen

Style's intrinsic qualities make it the Supreme Ultimate of the Supreme Ultimate.

Each of these is covered in its own section. DeMarco begins with a short overview of the Chinese cultural view of history and the confusions of authorship that arise from false attribution, deliberate or otherwise, that occur frequently in the Taiji Classics and other older literature on the martial arts. Despite the often confusing complexity of martial arts history, DeMarco says, a somewhat clear picture of Taiji development can emerge.

He begins his search for clarity with several older theories about the origins of Taiji that say the art could have appeared as long ago as 500 AD in Nanking, in Kiangsu Province. A competing theory, DeMarco says, places the origin a couple of hundred years later in the city now known as X'ian in Shensi Province—the same place where the famous Terra Cotta Warrior Army was unearthed. DeMarco likens these theories of pre-Chen development to the attribution of the Taiji Classics to the ancients: a move done to add prestige in a culture that venerates its ancestors.

Likewise, he dismisses the Chang Sanfeng legend, though at considerably greater length since he takes some time to relate several particulars of Chang's story. But Chang is, in the end, a fiction on which to hang the identity of Taiji, much as Bodhidharma has a similar function for Shaolin kung fu.

From here, DeMarco moves on to Chen Village, where the haziness of the myths and legends of Taiji history vanishes beneath the sunshine of recorded historical fact. These begin with a description of Chen Village not just as the place of origin for Taiji, but as a village in a very real sense, where people lived in a society that often experienced oppression. Thus the clan, and the group identity and protection it afforded, attained a high level of importance in the well-being of the self and family.

Wang Tsung-yueh gets his own critique as, if not founder of Taiji, at least as transmitter of a form of the art to Chen Village. DeMarco credits Wang with possibly linking the separate Thirteen Postures into Chang Chuan—Long Boxing—and of having an influence on Chen Village boxing. But he makes a distinction between Taiji's progenitors, like Chang Chuan, and the development of Taijiquan, which begins now, at Chen Village—specifically with Chen Wangting (aka Tsou T'ing, 1597–1664). Chen's original style was cobbled together, DeMarco says, from his village style, from training during his military career as he rose to the position of garrison commander, and from material he picked up in his travels. This is very much the Chen-centered Taiji origin story.

From here, DeMarco segues into the subject of clan secrecy regarding martial arts in general and Chen Family Taiji in particular. This moves on to an analysis of Chen style, which, remember, was little known in the West at the time. The analysis focuses on Chen's claim of originality and implies that the other styles—though not without merit—are really just watered down versions of Chen. He also breaks down the similarities and differences between Chen and other styles.

DeMarco then tours the Chen Family lineage, with thumbnail descriptions of major masters along the way. This continues up to the time of the writing, and it is easily the most detailed account of the Chen family I've seen. Individuals who learned Taiji from the Chens and later founded their own styles are treated in the next section. This, too, begins with a list of Chen masters but quickly moves on to the Wu brothers, founders of Wu/Hao style, and their students down through Li Yiyu and others to Sun Lutang, developer of his own syncretic style. The Yang Family style and its branches, such as Wu Family style, are covered next. This stuff is pretty much the standard history, but it enjoys a higher level of detail than almost any other similar account that I've seen in other sources, as befitting the booklet's academic bent.

The next section delves into the topic of secrecy surrounding the martial arts in general and Taiji in particular. This practice is shown to have its roots in paternal succession through sons—sometimes familial, sometimes chosen—who receive deeper, more specialized, and proprietary training. With regard to the martial arts, of course, there also is the issue of withholding the secrets of one's martial art so as not to give away an advantage.

DeMarco's analysis of secrecy within the Chen clan extends not just to outsiders but to clan members themselves. While most of the clan probably knew some Chen Taiji, only a select few knew the art truly and deeply. Tied up in all of this is the core family and the attempts by its members to improve their status within the family as well as within society at large. The section ends with a page or so on the special aspects of Chen Style. This material makes a few valid points, but these are embedded in some philosophical verbiage that, while not uninteresting, really isn't to the point. Anyway, as we all really know, it's the master not the method that really counts. Five pages of charts depicting various Taiji lineages close out the monograph.

Considering the historical information available at the time of its writing, DeMarco's monograph was a groundbreaking work and a sincere attempt to add clarity to Taiji history. In addition to providing one of the best histories of Taiji available at the time, it's also deep and interesting reading for those of us who like this sort of thing. I don't always agree with him, and while that's not the point, I think I'll go over a few of my disagreements anyway.

Foremost among them is that the monograph's premise is marred by its Chen-origin-centeredness. There was a tendency at the time of Chen style's introduction to the West to somewhat overblow Chen style's gravitas—not that it doesn't intrinsically have that. But I think that some of DeMarco's arguments are undermined by information we now know but that was not readily available at the time he wrote this. For example, DeMarco credits Wang Tsung-yueh with transmitting a sort of incomplete, Taiji-ish martial art to the Chen family, but the more popular story of Wang traveling through the region and teaching the Chen's Taiji is lent some credence by the remarkable similarity between the Taiji of Chen Village and that of nearby Zhaobao Village. While it is possible that Zhaobao's Taiji was learned from the Chens—and some advocate for this point of view—Zhaobao history denies that. So it's equally possible that Wang spent time in both villages as he moved through the province earning his living as an itinerant martial artist and spreading his Grand Ultimate martial art. There is no hard evidence either way, but the roots of Zhaobao Taiji are as shrouded in mystery as those of Chen Family style.

It also is very possible—likely, even—that Wang's Taiji was more fully developed than DeMarco credits. Wang must have been pretty proficient to have made his living as a martial artist and to have left such legacy, no matter what his actual role in the creation of Taiji. DeMarco also says that Wang named the art Taijiquan. But more recently, some historians attribute the establishment of the name Taijiquan—in lieu of Long Boxing, Chen Boxing, or the several other names by which the art was called—to one Ong Tong following a demonstration of Chen style by Yang Luchuan.[1]

As for the other styles of Taiji being simply watered-down versions of Chen, well, that's simply not true. They are simply different, though similar or related methods to manifest the same energies. Yang Chengfu, was a formidable opponent, and his uncle and the early Wu family masters were trainers of the imperial guard for a reason. The flavor might be different among different Taiji styles, but all of them rely on and embody the same principles. At the time that DeMarco wrote this paper, however, Chen's mystique was strong, and as the "original style," shouldn't it be the best? Even if Chen is truly excellent, not only is that attitude an example of the ancestor worship that DeMarco disparages earlier in the monograph for its tendency to obscure, it completely ignores the effects that centuries of subsequent development have had on Taiji. There is no golden age of Taiji somewhere in the past. The golden age of Taiji is right now.

But while I might argue with some of DeMarco's points, I think this is a valuable read. And I'll also say this about him: In 1992, six years after he published this groundbreaking monograph, he established and edited the groundbreaking *Journal of Asian Martial Arts*, which ran until 2012. This superlative journal, which was peer reviewed, was published in English, Spanish, and Greek. During its run, it garnered many awards, including one of the 10-Best Magazines of 1992 by *Library Journal*. DeMarco also published books, beginning with *Martial Musings: A Portrayal of the Martial Arts in the 20th Century*, a memoir by Robert W. Smith. (Reviewed in Volume I of this series.) I think all that speaks volumes for DeMarco's credibility. Although the journal is no longer being published, at the time of this writing, there is an active website where you can purchase individual articles for a modest fee. Also, collections of the journal are available from Amazon.

Notes
1 "Tai Chi." Wikipedia, https://en.wikipedia.org/wiki/Tai_chi

Li Li Ta Scrapbook

By Li Li Ta
(Students of Li Li Ta, 1982, 210 pages)

This homemade book with no real cover and no real title might be most properly described as a commemorative scrapbook. The "title page" reads, "This Compilation of Thoughts, Translations, Art from Lida Is a Living Tribute to Our Teacher and Friend." Li Li Ta, known to his students as Lida, was a San Francisco Bay Area artist, professional dancer, and Taiji teacher. Lida, sad to say, took his own life in 1982. Many people for many reasons choose that avenue of escape from this world. I've personally known too. many. I'm not them, so I can't say if they were right or not. All I can say is that we all die somehow, sometime. However and whenever we go is not really the point. It's how we lived and what we did.

For full disclosure, my Taiji practice began in early 1980 with students of Lida. I took a few workshops with him when he visited my hometown of Houston, but it was too early in my Taiji career to benefit from my few interactions with him as much as I might have if they'd occurred later. I practiced his form, which he'd learned from Wu Kungyi, exclusively for three years before his student and my teacher, Frieda Armstrong Fox, decided to take a break from teaching. I practiced for a couple of years longer on my own, then found a teacher of Northern Wu Style and learned that. I practiced the two concurrently for a couple of years, but then time constraints forced me to choose one or the other, and I chose Northern Wu for reasons not germane here.

So, I didn't know Lida, but I did have some interaction with him, and even more with a couple of his students other than Frieda. These students, who'd moved from Houston to Oakland to study directly with Lida, encouraged my wife and me to follow them, and we were on the verge of doing so when news of his suicide arrived. That put an end to our plans, but even more to the progress of his students. We were just planning. They were already invested, then abruptly left adrift. In an effort to come to terms with Lida's absence and the manner of it, they compiled this scrapbook. In a way, it is similar to Bruce Lee's *Tao of Jeet Kun Do*. I am in no way comparing Bruce Lee and Lida, either as martial artists or as men. But both books bear a similar genesis as the accumulated but not self-organized leavings of fertile and creative minds. Lee's book is no less a scrapbook than this one is.

Li Li Ta was born in China (location unknown to me) in 1922. He was educated at Fu Tan University in Shanghai, where he studied art and subsequently had several art exhibitions. He completed a course in Taiji at the Chien Chuan Taiji Chuan Institute in Shanghai in 1945. (This was the main Wu Family Taiji teaching center.) The next year, he was accepted as a disciple in the first group of disciples of Wu Kungyi, grandson and son, respectively, of Wu Style founders Wu Quanyu and Wu Chienchuan. For two years, he served as an instructor at the Chien Chuan Tai Chi Chuan Institute and assisted Wu Kungyi in giving lessons to advanced students, both in China and Hong Kong. He then continued as instructor at the institute and privately until 1968, at which time he moved to the San Francisco Bay Area.

While still in Hong Kong, he learned ballroom dancing from two English dancing masters—Stanley James and Jack McGregor (world champion of 1955)—and he taught ballroom dancing in Hong Kong for ten years before moving to the United States. No doubt his expertise in Taiji profoundly affected the character of his ballroom dancing. I saw him do a little during one of his trips to Houston, and his movements across the dance floor were smooth as silk. In the Bay Area, Lida made a splash on all three fronts: dancing, art, and Taiji. The scrapbook contains several of his resumes, which include lists of his numerous art shows and exhibitions. Following the the resumes are testimonials from four of his students and a newspaper article about him, written not long before his death.

The next section begins with a handwritten chart of Taiji's family tree. I have to say that Lida tended to use some obscure spellings for names. The surname "Chen," as in Chen style, is spelled, alternately, "Chang" and "Cheng." Yang Luchan comes out Yang Luchang. But no matter. A handwritten history is next. In it, Lida lists a number of historical figures, beginning with Chang Wong Ting (his spelling, apparently, of Chang Sanfeng) ca. 1644. Most of the fifteen entries, which end with Wu Kungyi, have notes regarding the individual's contribution to Taiji in general and Wu style specifically. The next thirty-six pages are occupied by single-sided class handouts of the type you might see given out in any Taiji class. Some tell what Taiji is, and some talk about Taiji's background, purpose, or methodology. And of course, there are form lists in various forms. Most interesting here to Taiji historians is a more detailed history of the genesis of Wu style. These pages obviously were a work in progress, for they contain numerous handwritten edits. In addition, the story is not told well. But the information is there if you don't mind the text jumping around a little.

Another chapter of interest to the general Taiji reader is "Ten Rules of Tai Chi," which is Lida's translation of material told by Yang Chengfu to Chen Weiming. (This also can be found in Paul Brennan's translation of Yang Cheng-fu/Chen Wei-ming's *Methods of Applying Taiji Boxing*, reviewed in Volume V of this series.)

After another student commemoration, Lida translates several of the Taiji Classics and provides extensive commentary on them. A history of Taiji is next, which begins with the standard Chang Sanfeng story. Fourteen pages on Lida's art, many of which are photocopied newspaper articles, come next, followed by several pages of short essays by Lida, and concluding with the curriculum for gaining a teaching certificate in Taiji from him. These are followed by many pages of flyers for his classes, demonstrations, and so forth. The book concludes with a photocopy of the official articles of incorporation for Lida's company, Taiji America.

This scrapbook is probably of interest primarily to Lida's students and, perhaps, historians of Taiji who might gain something from its relatively detailed history of the Wu family. The average Taiji reader might be interested in that, too, and in Lida's translations of Yang Chengfu and the Taiji Classics. Otherwise, while it contains this worthwhile material, most of the scrapbook consists of class handouts, and information on Lida as an artist, calligrapher, and dance instructor that would not be of interest to the average martial arts reader. As I said at the outset, this was published in a limited edition primarily for his students, so it is probably nearly impossible to find. I have one only because I am in the lineage, so to speak.

Phosphene Publishing Company
publishes books and DVDs relating to literature,
history, the paranormal, film, spirituality, and the
martial arts.

For other great titles, visit
phosphenepublishing.com

www.ingramcontent.com/pod-product-compliance
Lightning Source LLC
Chambersburg PA
CBHW050109170426
43198CB00014B/2509